The Sigma Male

Understanding and Navigating the World of the Independent Male

Gabriel Thornridge

CONTENTS

1. The Rise of the Sigma Male

1.1 The Evolution of Male Archetypes

The male archetype has evolved over time, with various societal changes and shifts in cultural norms leading to the emergence of new and different types of men. From the hunter-gatherer societies of our ancestors to the highly interconnected and globalized world of today, the concept of what it means to be a man has been constantly changing. In this chapter, we will explore the evolution of male archetypes, with a particular focus on the rise of the sigma male.

Historically, men have been expected to conform to a set of traditional gender roles. These roles were often based on physical strength, aggression, and dominance, and were seen as essential to the survival of society. For example, in hunter-gatherer societies, men were expected to be skilled hunters, protectors, and providers for their families. These roles were still prevalent throughout much of human history, with men expected to be the primary breadwinners and protectors of their families.

However, as societies became more complex and the roles of men began to shift, new archetypes began to emerge. In the 20th century, the emergence of the metrosexual, who embraced traditionally feminine traits like grooming and fashion, challenged traditional notions of masculinity. Similarly, the rise of the sensitive, emotionally aware man challenged the idea that men should be stoic and unemotional.

But perhaps the most significant shift in male archetypes in recent times has been the emergence of the sigma male. The sigma male is a unique and complex individual who defies traditional categorization. Unlike the alpha male, who is often seen as a dominant, aggressive leader, the sigma male is more of a lone wolf. He is independent, self-sufficient, and often operates outside of traditional social hierarchies.

The rise of the sigma male can be attributed to a number of factors. One of the most significant is the changing nature of work and employment. In the past, men were expected to work in traditional, hierarchical organizations and climb the corporate ladder. However, as the nature of work has changed, with the rise of the gig economy and remote work, new opportunities have emerged for independent-minded individuals who are comfortable working outside of traditional structures.

Another factor contributing to the rise of the sigma male is the changing nature of relationships and interpersonal dynamics. In the past, men were expected to conform to traditional gender roles in relationships, with men expected to be the dominant, breadwinning partner. However, as gender roles have become more fluid and egalitarian, men have had to adapt and find new ways of relating to their partners and the world around them.

The sigma male is also a product of changing cultural norms around masculinity. As traditional notions of masculinity have come under scrutiny, men have had to rethink what it means to be a man in the 21st century. The sigma male represents a new type of masculinity that values independence, self-sufficiency, and authenticity over traditional markers of success like wealth and status.

One of the defining characteristics of the sigma male is his ability to operate outside of traditional social hierarchies. Unlike the alpha male, who is often seen as the dominant leader of a social group, the sigma male is more of a lone wolf. He is independent, self-sufficient, and often operates on the periphery of social groups. This is not to say that the sigma male is antisocial or a loner; rather, he is someone who values his independence and autonomy above all else.

Another defining characteristic of the sigma male is his ability to thrive in uncertain and unpredictable environments. The sigma male is comfortable with uncertainty and is able to adapt quickly to changing circumstances. This makes him a valuable asset in today's rapidly changing and unpredictable world.

The sigma male is also highly self-sufficient and independent. He is comfortable being alone and does not rely on others for validation or approval. This independence allows him to pursue his goals and interests without being held back by the expectations or limitations of others.

One of the most important aspects of the sigma male is his authenticity. Unlike the alpha male, who is often seen as a caricature of masculinity, the sigma male is someone who is comfortable being true to himself. He is not interested in conforming to societal expectations or living up to traditional notions of success. Instead, he is focused on living a life that is meaningful and fulfilling to him.

The rise of the sigma male represents a major shift in our cultural understanding of masculinity. As traditional notions of gender roles and social hierarchies have been challenged, new archetypes have emerged that value independence, authenticity, and self-sufficiency over traditional markers of success. The sigma male is a product of these changing cultural norms, and represents a new type of masculinity that is adaptable, authentic, and independent. Whether or not the sigma male will continue to grow in popularity remains to be seen, but there is no doubt that he represents a significant shift in the way we think about what it means to be a man in the 21st century.

1.2 The Birth of the Sigma Male

The rise of the Sigma Male can be traced back to the mid-twentieth century when traditional gender roles began to shift. For centuries, men were expected to be providers and protectors while women were expected to be caretakers and homemakers. However, as the world became more industrialized, women began to enter the workforce in larger numbers, and men were no longer the sole breadwinners of their families.

As women gained more independence and equal rights, the traditional alpha male archetype began to lose its appeal. Men who were dominant and aggressive were no longer seen as the ideal partner, and a new type of male began to emerge - one who was independent, self-sufficient, and didn't conform to societal norms.

This new type of male was dubbed the Sigma Male, a term that was first coined by Vox Day in his book, The Return of the Great Depression. The Sigma Male is a man who does not fit into the traditional alpha or beta male categories. While he may have some alpha traits, such as confidence and assertiveness, he doesn't seek out dominance or control over others. Instead, he values his independence above all else and has a strong sense of self-reliance.

The birth of the Sigma Male can also be attributed to the rise of technology and the internet. With the advent of social media and online communities, men who previously felt isolated or misunderstood now had a platform to connect with others who shared their values and beliefs.

The Sigma Male is often drawn to online communities and forums where he can engage in intellectual discussions, share knowledge and ideas, and form meaningful connections with like-minded individuals. These communities provide a sense of belonging and acceptance that may be lacking in the real world.

Another factor that contributed to the rise of the Sigma Male is the changing nature of work. With the rise of the gig economy and remote work, many people are no longer tied to traditional 9-5 jobs. This has allowed Sigma Males to pursue their passions and interests without being confined to a specific career path or company.

Sigma Males are often entrepreneurs, freelancers, or self-employed individuals who value freedom and flexibility above all else. They are driven by their own personal goals and ambitions, rather than external validation or societal pressure.

The birth of the Sigma Male can also be seen as a response to the increasing pressure and expectations placed on men in modern society. Men are expected to be strong, stoic, and emotionally resilient, while also being sensitive and empathetic. These conflicting expectations can be difficult to navigate, and the Sigma Male offers an alternative way of being.

By rejecting societal norms and expectations, Sigma Males are able to create their own path in life and live according to their own values and beliefs. They are not bound by traditional gender roles or societal pressures, and can freely express themselves in ways that may be seen as unconventional or non-traditional.

In conclusion, the birth of the Sigma Male can be attributed to a combination of factors, including the shift in traditional gender roles, the rise of technology and the internet, the changing nature of work, and the increasing pressure and expectations placed on men in modern society. The Sigma Male offers an alternative way of being that is characterized by independence, self-reliance, and a rejection of societal norms and expectations. As the world continues to evolve and change, it is likely that the Sigma Male will continue to rise in prominence and influence.

1.3 From Outcast to Alpha: How the Sigma Male Rose to Prominence

The Sigma Male is a relatively new concept that has risen to prominence in recent times. While the Alpha Male has long been the dominant force in society, the Sigma Male has emerged as a new breed of independent male who has managed to break the mold and rise to prominence. In this chapter, we will explore how the Sigma Male went from being an outcast to becoming an Alpha in his own right.

The term Sigma Male was coined to define a type of man who is neither Alpha nor Beta. The Sigma Male is someone who is a lone wolf, but not necessarily because he wants to be. He is simply someone who does not conform to the traditional male hierarchy, and as a result, he is often seen as an outsider.

The Sigma Male may not have the same level of social skills as the Alpha Male, but he is highly independent and self-sufficient. He does not seek validation from others and is not afraid to go against the status quo. This makes him a highly respected and admired figure by those around him, even if he is not always in the spotlight.

The Sigma Male is often seen as a threat by Alpha Males, who feel that their dominance is being challenged. This is because the Sigma Male does not conform to the traditional male hierarchy, which is based on status, wealth, and power. Instead, he focuses on self-improvement and forging his own path in life.

The Sigma Male's rise to prominence can be attributed to a number of factors. Firstly, the changing nature of society has allowed for more individualism and less conformity. In the past, conformity was seen as a virtue, but today, people are encouraged to be themselves and pursue their own goals.

Secondly, the rise of social media has allowed for greater visibility and exposure for those who are not part of the traditional male hierarchy. The Sigma Male can now connect with others who share his values and beliefs, and he can build his own following and gain recognition for his achievements.

Thirdly, the Sigma Male's focus on self-improvement and independence has made him highly attractive to women. In a world where women are no longer dependent on men for financial security, they are looking for partners who can offer them emotional and intellectual stimulation, as well as genuine companionship. The Sigma Male's independence and self-sufficiency make him an ideal partner for many women, who are looking for someone who can challenge them intellectually and emotionally.

In conclusion, the rise of the Sigma Male is a reflection of the changing nature of society and the increasing emphasis on individualism and self-improvement. The Sigma Male has shown that it is possible to break free from the traditional male hierarchy and forge one's own path in life. While the Alpha Male may still be the dominant force in society, the Sigma Male has carved out his own niche and has become a respected and admired figure in his own right.

1.4 The Cultural Shift That Favored the Sigma Male

The cultural shift that favored the sigma male is a complex phenomenon that emerged in the late 20th century and has been gaining momentum ever since. It reflects a fundamental change in societal values and norms, and it has both positive and negative implications for men and women.

To understand this cultural shift, it's important to first define what we mean by the sigma male. The sigma male is an archetype of masculinity that is distinct from the alpha male and the beta male. Unlike the alpha, the sigma is not interested in dominating others or being the center of attention. Unlike the beta, the sigma is not interested in conforming to social norms or seeking approval from others. Instead, the sigma is an independent and self-reliant individual who values freedom, creativity, and authenticity above all else.

The rise of the sigma male can be traced back to several factors. One of the most important is the decline of traditional gender roles and the rise of feminism. As women have gained more opportunities and freedoms in society, men have had to reconsider their own roles and identities. The old model of masculinity, which emphasized dominance and aggression, no longer seemed relevant or desirable to many men.

Another factor in the rise of the sigma male is the growth of the knowledge economy and the decline of traditional manufacturing jobs. In the past, men could find meaning and purpose in their work as providers and protectors of their families. But as the economy has shifted away from manual labor and toward intellectual and creative work, men have had to find new sources of identity and fulfillment.

A third factor in the rise of the sigma male is the growth of the internet and social media. These technologies have enabled people to connect and communicate in new ways, and have created new opportunities for self-expression and creativity. For many sigma males, the internet has been a lifeline, allowing them to find like-minded individuals and build communities based on shared interests and values.

The cultural shift that has favored the sigma male has had both positive and negative effects. On the one hand, it has allowed men to explore new forms of masculinity that are more authentic and fulfilling. Men are no longer constrained by traditional gender roles and can pursue careers and lifestyles that are more in line with their personal values and aspirations.

On the other hand, the rise of the sigma male has also created new challenges and dilemmas. For one thing, many men feel lost and adrift in a world that no longer provides clear guidelines or role models for masculinity. They may struggle to find a sense of purpose or meaning in their lives, and may feel disconnected from others and from society as a whole.

Another challenge of the sigma male is that their independence and self-reliance can sometimes lead to isolation and loneliness. While sigma males value freedom and autonomy, they also need meaningful connections with others in order to thrive. Finding a balance between independence and interdependence can be a difficult task, and one that requires a great deal of self-awareness and self-reflection.

Despite these challenges, the cultural shift that has favored the sigma male is likely to continue in the years ahead. As society becomes more complex and diverse, people will need to find new ways of navigating the world and defining themselves. The sigma male offers one possible model of masculinity that is flexible, adaptable, and attuned to the needs of the individual.

Ultimately, whether the rise of the sigma male is a positive or negative trend depends on how it is embraced and enacted by individuals and society as a whole. If sigma males can find ways to balance their independence and self-reliance with a sense of connection and community, they may be able to create a new model of masculinity that is both fulfilling and sustainable. If not, they risk becoming isolated and disconnected from the world around them. The choice is theirs.

1.5 The Sigma Male's Impact on Society and Culture

The Sigma Male's Impact on Society and Culture

The rise of the Sigma Male has had a significant impact on society and culture. This unique personality type has challenged traditional notions of masculinity and has brought about a new way of thinking about what it means to be a man. In this section, we will examine the ways in which Sigma Males have impacted society and culture and explore the implications of their rise.

Firstly, Sigma Males have challenged the traditional model of masculinity. Sigma Males reject the alpha male hierarchy, which values aggression, dominance, and competition. Instead, Sigma Males value independence, self-reliance, and autonomy. This different approach to masculinity has challenged the traditional notion that men should be aggressive and dominant. Sigma Males have shown that there are other ways of being a man, and that a lack of aggression and dominance does not make a man weak.

Secondly, Sigma Males have brought about a new way of thinking about relationships. Sigma Males value their independence and do not need to be in a relationship to feel fulfilled. Instead, they prioritize their own goals and desires. This approach to relationships challenges the traditional notion that men need to be in a relationship to feel complete. Sigma Males have shown that it is possible to be happy and fulfilled without being in a relationship.

Thirdly, Sigma Males have challenged the traditional model of success. Sigma Males do not measure success by traditional markers such as wealth, power, or status. Instead, they measure success by their own personal goals and achievements. This approach challenges the traditional notion that success is defined by material possessions or societal status. Sigma Males have shown that success can be defined on an individual level and that there is no one-size-fits-all definition of success.

Fourthly, Sigma Males have challenged the traditional model of work. Sigma Males do not conform to the traditional model of work, which values conformity, obedience, and subservience. Instead, Sigma Males prioritize their own goals and desires and are not afraid to pursue unconventional career paths. This approach challenges the traditional notion that work should be a means to an end and that one should sacrifice their own desires for the sake of a career.

Lastly, Sigma Males have impacted culture by challenging the traditional models of gender roles. Sigma Males reject the traditional notion that men should be breadwinners and women should be caretakers. Instead, they value independence and autonomy and do not conform to traditional gender roles. This approach challenges the traditional notion that men and women should conform to specific gender roles and has contributed to a more gender-fluid culture.

The impact of Sigma Males on society and culture has been significant. They have challenged traditional notions of masculinity, relationships, success, work, and gender roles. Their rise has shown that there is no one-size-fits-all approach to life and that it is possible to live a fulfilling and successful life without conforming to societal norms. The rise of the Sigma Male has contributed to a more diverse and inclusive society and has challenged the traditional models of masculinity and gender roles.

2. Characteristics of the Sigma Male

2.1 Sigma Males are Independent Thinkers

Sigma males are often referred to as independent thinkers, and for good reason. These men tend to be highly analytical, introspective, and self-aware, which allows them to think critically about the world around them and come to their own conclusions about various topics. They are not afraid to challenge the status quo or go against popular opinion if they believe it is the right thing to do.

One of the key traits of the sigma male is their ability to think independently. They are not swayed by public opinion or social pressure, and instead rely on their own intuition and reasoning to make decisions. This does not mean that sigma males are closed-minded or unwilling to listen to other perspectives, but rather that they are selective about the information they take in and how they process it.

Sigma males tend to have a deep sense of self-awareness and introspection, which allows them to understand their own thoughts, emotions, and motivations. This introspective nature also makes them highly attuned to the world around them, and they are often able to pick up on details and nuances that others may miss. This attention to detail and ability to see the bigger picture makes them excellent problem solvers and critical thinkers.

One of the reasons that sigma males are so independent in their thinking is that they are not easily influenced by external factors. They do not seek validation from others or feel the need to conform to societal norms or expectations. Instead, they are guided by their own values, principles, and beliefs, which they have developed through their own experiences and observations.

This independence of thought can sometimes make sigma males appear aloof or detached from others, but this is not the case. They are simply more selective about the people they surround themselves with, preferring those who share their values and interests. They are not interested in superficial connections or small talk, but instead seek out deep, meaningful relationships with like-minded individuals.

Sigma males are also highly adaptable and flexible in their thinking. They are not wedded to any particular ideology or belief system, and are willing to change their minds if presented with compelling evidence or arguments. This openness to new ideas and perspectives allows them to grow and evolve over time, rather than becoming stagnant or stuck in their ways.

Another key characteristic of the sigma male is their ability to think outside the box. They are not content with conventional wisdom or the status quo, and instead seek out new and innovative solutions to problems. This creative and entrepreneurial spirit makes them natural leaders and innovators, who are not afraid to take calculated risks and try new things.

This independent thinking also makes sigma males highly resistant to groupthink or herd mentality. They are not swayed by peer pressure or the desire to fit in, and instead rely on their own instincts and analysis to make decisions. This can sometimes put them at odds with others, but they are comfortable standing alone if they believe they are doing the right thing.

Overall, sigma males are independent thinkers who rely on their own intuition, analysis, and values to make decisions. They are not swayed by external factors or societal norms, but instead rely on their own unique perspective and introspection to navigate the world around them. This independence of thought can sometimes make them appear aloof or detached, but in reality, they are deeply attuned to the world around them and seek out meaningful connections with like-minded individuals.

2.2 Sigma Males are Introverted by Nature

The Sigma Male: Understanding and Navigating the World of the Independent Male is a book that delves deep into the psyche of the enigmatic Sigma Male. The Sigma Male is a rare breed of men who stand out from the crowd due to their independent nature, self-confidence, and unconventional thinking. They do not conform to the norms of society and prefer to carve out their own path in life.

One of the key characteristics of a Sigma Male is their introverted nature. Sigma Males are not necessarily shy, but they tend to be reserved and introspective. They are not the life of the party, but they are excellent observers of human behavior. Sigma Males are not interested in superficial conversations, small talk, or gossip. They prefer deep, meaningful conversations with individuals who share their interests, visions, and values.

Sigma Males are not antisocial, but they do not crave social interaction as much as other men. They value their time and prefer to spend it doing things that they are passionate about. They do not need constant validation from others or seek approval from society. They are comfortable being alone and find solace in their own thoughts, ideas, and company.

Sigma Males are not attention seekers, and they do not feel the need to be the center of attention. They are happy being in the background and observing the world around them. They are not interested in seeking approval from others or conforming to societal expectations. They know who they are and what they stand for, and they do not need validation from others to feel secure.

Sigma Males are not averse to social interaction, but they are selective in their social circle. They prefer to have a few close friends who understand them and share their vision. They do not crave large social gatherings or parties, but they enjoy spending time with individuals who share their interests and passions. Sigma Males are excellent listeners and observers, and they value deep, meaningful conversations over shallow small talk.

Sigma Males are not emotionally disconnected, but they do not wear their emotions on their sleeves. They are not prone to emotional outbursts or mood swings, and they prefer to keep their emotions in check. They are comfortable with their emotions and do not feel the need to express them in a public setting. They prefer to deal with their emotions in private and do not seek validation or sympathy from others.

Sigma Males are not afraid to assert themselves when necessary, but they do not crave power or control. They are not interested in seeking leadership roles or dominating others. They prefer to work independently, and they are comfortable making decisions on their own. They do not need validation or approval from others to feel confident in their abilities.

Sigma Males are not averse to change, but they do not conform to societal norms. They are not interested in following the crowd and doing what everyone else is doing. They prefer to carve out their own path in life and are comfortable taking risks. They are not afraid of failure and see it as a learning opportunity.

In conclusion, Sigma Males are introverted by nature. They prefer to spend their time alone or in the company of individuals who share their interests and passions. They are not interested in seeking validation or approval from society and prefer to carve out their own path in life. They are comfortable being who they are and do not conform to societal expectations. Sigma Males are complex individuals with many layers, and their introverted nature is just one aspect of their character. Understanding and navigating the world of the Sigma Male requires an open mind and a willingness to embrace their unique qualities.

2.3 Sigma Males are Observant and Analytical

The Sigma Male is a unique individual who stands out from the crowd due to his independent nature and unconventional way of living life. One of the defining characteristics of the Sigma Male is his ability to observe and analyze his surroundings, making him an excellent problem solver and critical thinker. In this chapter, we will explore the observation and analytical skills of the Sigma Male, and how they contribute to his overall success.

Firstly, let's define what it means to be observant. Observance is the act of paying attention to one's surroundings and taking note of details that others may miss. Sigma Males are naturally observant individuals who have a keen eye for detail. They are always aware of their surroundings and can quickly pick up on changes and anomalies.

Observation skills are essential in many aspects of life, from personal relationships to professional settings. In social situations, Sigma Males can easily read body language and understand the emotions of those around them. This makes them great listeners and empathetic individuals who can build meaningful connections with others.

In the workplace, observation skills are equally essential. Sigma Males can quickly assess a situation and identify potential issues or areas for improvement. This makes them excellent problem solvers who can come up with creative solutions to complex problems.

Observation skills are particularly valuable in fields such as science and engineering, where attention to detail is critical. Sigma Males who work in these fields can quickly identify patterns and anomalies in data, leading to breakthroughs in research and development.

Next, let's explore the analytical skills of the Sigma Male. Analytical skills refer to an individual's ability to break down complex problems into smaller, more manageable parts. Sigma Males are excellent analytical thinkers who can quickly dissect problems and come up with effective solutions.

Analytical skills are particularly valuable in fields such as finance and business, where complex data analysis is needed. Sigma Males who work in these fields can quickly analyze financial data and identify trends that others may miss. This makes them valuable assets to their teams and organizations.

Analytical skills are also essential in personal life. Sigma Males can easily identify areas of their life that need improvement and come up with a plan to make changes. This makes them self-aware individuals who are always striving for personal growth.

Finally, let's explore how observation and analytical skills work together to make the Sigma Male a unique and successful individual. Sigma Males are not just observers; they are critical thinkers who can quickly analyze the information they gather. This makes them excellent decision-makers who can weigh the pros and cons of a situation and come up with the best course of action.

In the workplace, Sigma Males can quickly identify areas of their job that need improvement and come up with creative solutions to solve problems. They can also analyze data and make informed decisions that benefit their team and organization.

In personal life, Sigma Males can use their observation and analytical skills to assess their relationships and identify areas that need improvement. They can also use these skills to identify personal habits or behaviors that may be holding them back and make changes to improve their lives.

In conclusion, observation and analytical skills are essential characteristics of the Sigma Male. These skills make them excellent problem solvers, critical thinkers, and decision-makers. Sigma Males who use their observation and analytical skills effectively can achieve great success in all areas of their lives.

2.4 Sigma Males are Highly Adaptable

The Sigma Male is a personality type that is often misunderstood and overlooked in society. They are often seen as mysterious and enigmatic, and their characteristics are not as widely known as other personality types such as Alpha or Beta males. However, one of the key characteristics of the Sigma Male is their adaptability.

Adaptability is the ability to adjust to new circumstances or conditions and is an essential trait in today's fast-paced and ever-changing world. The Sigma Male possesses this ability in abundance and is capable of adapting to any situation or environment, whether it is a new job, a new city, or a new relationship.

One of the reasons for their adaptability is their independent nature. Sigma Males are not reliant on others and are often self-sufficient, which allows them to be more flexible in adapting to new situations. They are not tied down by social structures or hierarchies and can easily move between different social groups and environments.

Another reason for their adaptability is their introspective nature. Sigma Males are often deep thinkers and are constantly analyzing their surroundings and environment. This introspection allows them to be more aware of their strengths and weaknesses, which in turn helps them to adjust to new situations and environments.

Furthermore, Sigma Males possess a strong sense of self-awareness, which makes them more adaptable. They are well aware of their limitations, which allows them to be more open-minded and receptive to new ideas and concepts. They are not afraid to challenge their own beliefs and are always willing to learn and grow.

The adaptability of the Sigma Male is also reflected in their approach to problem-solving. They are not bound by traditional methods or solutions and are often able to come up with innovative and creative solutions to problems. They are not afraid to think outside the box and are always looking for new ways to improve themselves and their circumstances.

Moreover, the Sigma Male is not easily deterred by failure or setbacks. They view failure as an opportunity to learn and grow, and are always willing to take risks and try new things. This resilience allows them to adapt to any situation and overcome any obstacles that may come their way.

In conclusion, the adaptability of the Sigma Male is a key characteristic that sets them apart from other personality types. Their independence, introspection, self-awareness, problem-solving skills, and resilience make them highly adaptable to any situation or environment. This adaptability allows them to navigate the world with ease and achieve success in their professional and personal lives. It is important for society to recognize and value the unique qualities of the Sigma Male, as they have much to offer in terms of innovation, creativity, and resilience.

2.5 Sigma Males Value Their Freedom Above All Else

The Sigma Male is an enigmatic personality type that is often misunderstood. They are characterized as being independent and self-reliant individuals who value their freedom above all else. Unlike the Alpha Male, who seeks to dominate and control others, the Sigma Male prefers to operate on the fringes of society, carving out their own path and living life on their own terms.

One of the defining characteristics of the Sigma Male is their fierce commitment to personal freedom. They are fiercely independent and do not conform to societal norms or expectations. They march to the beat of their own drum and are unapologetic about it.

This desire for freedom is not limited to the physical realm, but also extends to their thoughts and beliefs. They value their intellectual independence and are not easily swayed by the opinions of others. They do not conform to the herd mentality and are not afraid to challenge conventional wisdom.

This intellectual independence is what sets the Sigma Male apart from other personality types. They are critical thinkers who are not afraid to question authority or challenge the status quo. They are not easily influenced by propaganda, and are adept at seeing through the spin that is often peddled by those in power.

The Sigma Male's fierce commitment to personal freedom has its roots in their desire for autonomy. They do not like to be told what to do, and will go to great lengths to maintain their independence. They do not like to be micromanaged or controlled, and will rebel against any attempt to do so.

In the workplace, the Sigma Male is often seen as a lone wolf. They work best when given the freedom to pursue their own projects and ideas. They do not like to be part of a team or be told how to do their job. They prefer to work independently and will seek out careers that allow them to do so.

This desire for autonomy extends to their personal lives as well. The Sigma Male values their privacy and will go to great lengths to protect it. They do not like to be tied down by relationships or obligations, and will often choose to remain single or have few close relationships.

This independence can be both a blessing and a curse for the Sigma Male. On the one hand, they are free to pursue their own interests and passions without having to answer to anyone. They are not burdened by the expectations of society or the opinions of others. On the other hand, this independence can lead to feelings of isolation and loneliness.

The Sigma Male's commitment to freedom is not limited to themselves, but also extends to others. They value individual liberty and are passionate about defending it. They are often champions of free speech, civil liberties, and human rights.

This commitment to freedom is what sets the Sigma Male apart from other personality types. They are not content to simply live their lives according to the rules and expectations of society. They see themselves as part of a larger struggle for freedom and will fight for it with all their might.

In conclusion, the Sigma Male is an independent and self-reliant personality type that values their freedom above all else. They are fiercely committed to personal autonomy and are not easily swayed by the opinions of others. They are critical thinkers who are not afraid to challenge authority or question the status quo. They are champions of individual liberty and are passionate about defending it. While this commitment to freedom can lead to feelings of isolation and loneliness, it is also what sets the Sigma Male apart from other personality types and makes them a force to be reckoned with in the world.

2.6 Sigma Males are Not Easily Influenced by Others

Sigma males are individuals who are self-sufficient, independent, and have a high level of emotional intelligence. They are often seen as aloof and mysterious, and their behavior can sometimes be misinterpreted as arrogance or standoffishness. However, there is more to the Sigma male than meets the eye.

One of the defining characteristics of the Sigma male is their ability to resist the influence of others. Sigma males are not easily swayed by peer pressure, societal norms, or the opinions of others. They have a strong sense of self and are not afraid to go against the grain if it means staying true to their own beliefs and values.

This ability to resist outside influence is rooted in the Sigma male's strong sense of independence. They are not interested in conforming to the expectations of others or fitting in with a particular group. Instead, they prefer to chart their own course and make decisions based on their own internal compass.

This independence can sometimes be mistaken for stubbornness or a lack of cooperation. However, Sigma males are not opposed to working with others or collaborating on projects. They simply prefer to do so on their own terms, and in a way that maintains their autonomy and individuality.

Another factor that contributes to the Sigma male's resistance to outside influence is their emotional intelligence. Sigma males are highly attuned to their own emotions, as well as the emotions of others. They are able to recognize when someone is trying to manipulate or influence them, and are able to resist these efforts with ease.

This emotional intelligence also allows Sigma males to navigate social situations with ease. They are able to read the room and adjust their behavior accordingly, which often means keeping a low profile and observing from the sidelines. This ability to blend in while maintaining their independence is a hallmark of the Sigma male.

Despite their ability to resist influence, Sigma males are not immune to the effects of their surroundings. They are highly sensitive to their environment, and can be deeply affected by negative people or situations. However, they are able to recognize when their environment is toxic and take steps to remove themselves from it.

In addition, Sigma males are not opposed to seeking out guidance or advice when they need it. However, they are selective about who they turn to for help. They prefer to seek out trusted sources who have proven themselves to be reliable and trustworthy.

Overall, the ability to resist influence is a critical trait for the Sigma male. It allows them to maintain their independence and autonomy, while also navigating the complex social dynamics of the world around them. While this trait can sometimes be misunderstood or mistaken for arrogance, it is an essential part of the Sigma male's identity and should be celebrated as such.

2.7 Sigma Males Tend to Be Non-Conformist

The Sigma Male is a type of man who is often characterized as independent and self-sufficient. It is a personality type that is often misunderstood and misinterpreted, and this can be attributed to the fact that Sigma males tend to be non-conformist. They have a way of thinking that is different from that of the average person, and they do not subscribe to the conventional ways of the society.

Sigma males are independent thinkers who prefer to do things in their own way. They are not a part of any social group or clique, and they do not feel the need to conform to the expectations of society. They march to the beat of their own drum, and they have their own set of values and beliefs that guide their actions.

One of the defining characteristics of a Sigma Male is their non-conformity. They do not follow the norms and conventions of society, and they have a tendency to question everything. They are not afraid to challenge the status quo, and they have a unique perspective on the world.

Sigma males are often seen as rebellious and contrarian. They are not afraid to challenge authority or speak their minds, even if it means going against the majority. They have a strong sense of individualism, and they do not like to be told what to do. They are not easily swayed by peer pressure or societal norms, and they are not concerned with fitting in with the crowd. Instead, they focus on achieving their own goals and living life on their own terms.

One of the reasons why Sigma males are non-conformist is because they value their independence above all else. They do not like to be tied down by rules or regulations, and they value their freedom and autonomy. They have a strong sense of self-reliance, and they prefer to rely on themselves rather than others. This can often make them appear aloof or detached, but it is simply a reflection of their desire for independence.

Another reason why Sigma males are non-conformist is because they are often misunderstood by others. They have a unique perspective on the world, and they do not fit neatly into any predefined categories. They are often seen as mysterious or enigmatic, and this can make it difficult for them to connect with others. As a result, they tend to keep to themselves and avoid social situations where they feel they will not be understood.

Sigma males are also non-conformist in their career choices. They are not afraid to pursue unconventional paths, even if it means going against the expectations of society. They have a strong sense of ambition, and they are willing to take risks in order to achieve their goals. They are often entrepreneurs or freelancers, and they prefer to work for themselves rather than for someone else.

In relationships, Sigma males are also non-conformist. They do not follow the traditional dating norms, and they prefer to take things at their own pace. They are not interested in playing games or following the rules of the dating game. Instead, they prefer to be honest and straightforward about their intentions, and they do not like to be pressured into any kind of commitment. They value their freedom, and they are not interested in settling down until they find someone who truly understands and accepts them for who they are.

In conclusion, Sigma males tend to be non-conformist because they have a unique perspective on the world and a strong desire for independence. They are not afraid to challenge the norms and conventions of society, and they have a rebellious streak that sets them apart from the crowd. They are independent thinkers who value their autonomy above all else, and they are not interested in fitting in with the expectations of others. While their non-conformist tendencies may be misunderstood by some, they are simply a reflection of their desire to live life on their own terms.

2.8 Sigma Males Prefer to Work Alone or in Small Groups

The Sigma Male is a unique and distinct personality type that has been gaining recognition in recent years. The Sigma Male is an independent, self-sufficient, and highly individualistic individual. They are not interested in conforming to society's expectations, and they value their freedom and independence above all else. One of the defining characteristics of the Sigma Male is their preference for working alone or in small groups.

Sigma Males are highly self-sufficient individuals who prefer to work independently. They do not enjoy being micromanaged or having their work scrutinized by others. They prefer to work on their own terms and in their own way. Sigma Males are highly analytical and detail-oriented, and they are able to work through complex problems on their own.

Sigma Males are also highly individualistic, which means that they are not interested in conforming to the group mentality. They value their freedom and independence, and they are not interested in being part of a team or group that restricts their autonomy. This does not mean that Sigma Males are anti-social or incapable of working with others. However, they prefer to work in small groups or with individuals who share their values and work ethic.

Working in small groups allows Sigma Males to maintain their autonomy while still benefiting from the input and perspectives of others. Small groups also allow Sigma Males to maintain a high level of control over their work and to ensure that their contributions are recognized and valued. Sigma Males are highly competitive individuals, and they thrive on the recognition and respect that comes from excelling in their work.

Sigma Males are also highly focused individuals who are able to work for long periods of time without getting distracted. They are able to concentrate on complex tasks for hours on end, which makes them highly productive workers. However, Sigma Males are also highly introspective individuals who need time to reflect on their work and their goals. They prefer to work in environments that allow them to have this time for reflection, and they are not comfortable in environments that are overly chaotic or noisy.

Another reason why Sigma Males prefer to work alone or in small groups is that they have a high need for privacy. Sigma Males are highly guarded individuals who do not like to reveal too much about themselves to others. They are not interested in small talk or idle chitchat, and they prefer to keep their thoughts and feelings to themselves. Working alone or in small groups allows Sigma Males to maintain a high level of privacy and to avoid the social pressure that comes with being part of a larger group.

Sigma Males are also highly independent individuals who do not like to rely on others for support. They are not interested in hierarchical structures or in being part of a larger organization. They prefer to work on their own terms and to pursue their own goals. Working alone or in small groups allows Sigma Males to maintain their independence and to avoid the restrictions that come with being part of a larger organization.

Finally, Sigma Males prefer to work alone or in small groups because they are highly self-motivated individuals. They do not need external validation or encouragement to pursue their goals. They have a strong inner drive that propels them forward, and they are able to motivate themselves to achieve their goals. Working alone or in small groups allows Sigma Males to tap into this inner drive and to pursue their goals with a high level of intensity and focus.

In conclusion, Sigma Males are highly individualistic and self-sufficient individuals who prefer to work alone or in small groups. They value their freedom and independence, and they are not interested in conforming to the group mentality. Working alone or in small groups allows Sigma Males to maintain their autonomy, privacy, and independence while still benefiting from the input and perspectives of others. It also allows Sigma Males to tap into their strong inner drive and to pursue their goals with a high level of intensity and focus. Understanding and navigating the world of the Sigma Male requires an appreciation for their unique personality type and an acceptance of their preference for working alone or in small groups.

2.9 Sigma Males Are Driven by Their Passions

Sigma Males are Driven by Their Passions

Sigma Males are often seen as enigmatic and elusive figures. They are known for their independence and their ability to navigate the world on their own terms. While they may seem aloof and disinterested, there is one thing that drives Sigma Males more than anything else: their passions.

Passions are what motivate Sigma Males to push the boundaries and challenge the status quo. They are the driving force behind their relentless pursuit of excellence and their refusal to conform to societal norms. Whether it's a love of music, art, literature, or science, Sigma Males are always chasing after their passions with an unrelenting determination.

One of the defining characteristics of Sigma Males is their ability to think outside the box. They are unconventional thinkers who are not afraid to take risks and try new things. This mindset is especially evident in their pursuit of their passions. Sigma Males are not content to simply dabble in their interests; they immerse themselves in them completely. They seek out new experiences and challenges, and they are always looking for ways to push themselves to new heights.

This relentless pursuit of passion often leads Sigma Males to excel in their chosen fields. They are not satisfied with mediocrity or conformity; they strive for excellence in everything they do. This drive and determination can be seen in the way they approach their work, their hobbies, and their relationships. Sigma Males are not content to simply go through the motions; they want to make a meaningful impact on the world around them.

In many ways, Sigma Males are similar to the archetype of the "mad scientist." They are passionate, driven individuals who are willing to take risks and challenge existing beliefs. They are not afraid to question authority or challenge established norms. This mindset can be seen in the way they approach their passions. Whether it's developing new technology or creating art that pushes the boundaries of traditional forms, Sigma Males are always looking for ways to innovate and push the limits of what is possible.

Another key aspect of Sigma Males' passion is their ability to focus intensely on their interests. They are not easily distracted or swayed by outside influences. When they are pursuing a particular goal or project, they become completely absorbed in it. They are able to block out distractions and focus all of their energy on the task at hand. This level of focus and dedication is what allows Sigma Males to achieve great things in their chosen fields.

Sigma Males' passion is also evident in the way they approach relationships. While they may not be as social or outgoing as other personality types, they are deeply committed to the people they care about. They may have a small circle of friends or family members, but they are fiercely loyal to those individuals. Their passion for their loved ones is evident in the way they prioritize their relationships and invest their time and energy into nurturing them.

One of the challenges that Sigma Males face is finding the right balance between their passions and other aspects of their lives. Because they are so driven by their interests, they may neglect other areas of their lives, such as their health or their relationships. It is important for Sigma Males to find ways to integrate their passions into their overall lifestyle without sacrificing other important aspects of their lives.

In order to do this, Sigma Males need to be intentional about setting boundaries and priorities. They need to recognize that their passions are an important part of who they are, but they should not overshadow other aspects of their lives. By setting realistic goals and managing their time effectively, Sigma Males can find a healthy balance between their passions and other responsibilities.

Another important aspect of managing their passions is understanding that failure is a natural part of the process. Sigma Males may become frustrated or discouraged when they encounter setbacks or obstacles in pursuit of their goals. However, it is important for them to remember that failure is not a reflection of their worth as a person. Instead, it is an opportunity to learn and grow from their experiences.

In conclusion, Sigma Males are driven by their passions, which are the driving force behind their relentless pursuit of excellence and their refusal to conform to societal norms. They are unconventional thinkers who are not afraid to take risks and try new things. Their passion is evident in the way they approach their work, their hobbies, and their relationships. However, it is important for Sigma

Males to find a healthy balance between their passions and other aspects of their lives, and to recognize that failure is a natural part of the process. By doing so, they can achieve great things and make a meaningful impact on the world around them.

2.10 Sigma Males Seek Authenticity in All Areas of Life.

Sigma Males Seek Authenticity in All Areas of Life

Sigma males are known for their independent and self-sufficient nature. They are often seen as loners or outsiders, but this is because they value their freedom and individuality. Sigma males seek authenticity in all areas of life, and they are not afraid to go against the norm if it means staying true to themselves.

Authenticity is a core value for sigma males, and they strive to be genuine in all their actions and interactions. They believe in being true to themselves, their beliefs, and their values. This means that they do not compromise their integrity or authenticity for anyone or anything. Sigma males are not interested in fitting in or conforming to societal norms or expectations. Instead, they focus on being true to themselves, even if it means going against the grain.

Sigma males are also honest and transparent in their relationships. They value honesty and transparency and believe that these qualities are essential for building trust and respect in relationships. They are not afraid to speak their minds or express their opinions, even if they are unpopular. Sigma males are not interested in playing games or being manipulative in their relationships. They believe that honesty and authenticity are the keys to building strong and meaningful relationships.

In their professional lives, sigma males seek authenticity by pursuing careers that align with their values and interests. They are not interested in jobs that are solely focused on making money or climbing the corporate ladder. Instead, they want to do work that is meaningful and fulfilling to them. Sigma males are often drawn to careers that allow them to work independently, such as entrepreneurship, freelancing, or consulting. They value their freedom and autonomy in their work and want to be able to make their own decisions and set their own schedules.

Sigma males also seek authenticity in their personal lives by pursuing hobbies and interests that they are passionate about. They are not interested in doing things just because they are popular or trendy. Instead, they want to do things that they genuinely enjoy and that bring them fulfillment. They may have unique hobbies or interests that others may find unusual or unconventional, but they do not care about what others think. Sigma males are comfortable with who they are and do not feel the need to conform to societal expectations.

Sigma males also seek authenticity in their personal relationships. They value deep and meaningful connections with others and do not settle for surface-level relationships. They want to connect with people on a deeper level and have conversations that are thought-provoking and meaningful. Sigma males are not interested in small talk or shallow conversations. They want to get to know people on a deeper level and understand what makes them tick.

Authenticity is not just a core value for sigma males, but it is also a way of life. They believe in being true to themselves, their beliefs, and their values, even if it means going against the norm. They do not compromise their integrity or authenticity for anyone or anything. Sigma males are honest, transparent, and genuine in their actions and interactions. They value deep and meaningful connections in their personal and professional relationships and pursue careers and hobbies that align with their values and interests.

In conclusion, sigma males seek authenticity in all areas of life. They value honesty, transparency, and genuine connections in their relationships. They pursue careers and hobbies that align with their values and interests, and they do not compromise their integrity or authenticity for anyone or anything. Authenticity is a way of life for sigma males, and they believe in being true to themselves, even if it means going against the norm.

3. The Sigma Male in Relationships

3.1 The Importance of Independence in Relationships

The Sigma male is someone who is independent and enjoys their solitude. They are not afraid to walk away from a relationship if it is not meeting their needs. However, this does not mean that they do not value relationships or the people in them. In fact, they are often fiercely loyal to those they care about. The importance of independence in relationships cannot be overstated, especially for Sigma males.

One of the main reasons independence is so important is that it allows individuals to maintain their sense of self. When two people come together in a relationship, it is easy to lose oneself in the other person's desires and expectations. This can lead to feeling suffocated and trapped, which is not a healthy environment for anyone. Sigma males understand this and value their independence because it allows them to maintain their sense of self.

Another reason independence is important is that it allows for personal growth. In a relationship, it is easy to become complacent and stop challenging oneself. Independence allows individuals to take risks and try new things without fear of judgment or consequence. This can lead to personal growth and development, which is essential for a fulfilling life.

Independence also allows for healthy boundaries. In a relationship, it is important to set boundaries and communicate them effectively.

Sigma males understand this and value their independence because it allows them to set and maintain healthy boundaries. This can lead to a stronger and more fulfilling relationship because both parties feel respected and understood.

Moreover, independence fosters creativity, which is essential for a healthy relationship. Creativity allows individuals to approach problems in unique ways and find solutions that work for them. Sigma males value their independence because it allows them to be creative and find new ways to approach problems in their relationships. This can lead to a more fulfilling and meaningful relationship.

Finally, independence is crucial for maintaining a healthy relationship because it allows individuals to be happy on their own. It is important to be happy with oneself before entering into a relationship. Sigma males understand this and value their independence because it allows them to be happy on their own. This can lead to a more fulfilling and loving relationship because both parties are happy and content with themselves.

In conclusion, the importance of independence in relationships cannot be overstated, especially for Sigma males. Independence allows individuals to maintain their sense of self, fosters personal growth, allows for healthy boundaries, fosters creativity, and is crucial for maintaining a healthy relationship. Sigma males value their independence because it allows them to be happy on their own and fosters personal growth and development. It is important to remember that independence does not mean isolation or a lack of love for others. Rather, it is a way to maintain a strong sense of self while still valuing and loving those around us.

3.2 Communicating as a Sigma Male

The Sigma Male is known for his independence and self-reliance, but this doesn't mean he doesn't communicate effectively. In fact, communicating as a Sigma Male requires a level of authenticity that many other personalities struggle to achieve.

One of the hallmarks of the Sigma Male is his ability to be honest and straightforward with others. He doesn't beat around the bush or sugarcoat things, but he also doesn't come across as rude or insensitive. Instead, he communicates his thoughts and feelings in a clear and concise manner, which helps avoid any misunderstandings or confusion.

This direct communication style can be particularly useful in romantic relationships, where honesty and transparency are essential for building trust and intimacy. The Sigma Male is not afraid to express his needs and desires, and he expects the same from his partner.

However, communicating as a Sigma Male can also be challenging, especially when dealing with more emotional or sensitive topics. The Sigma Male is not always comfortable with expressing his emotions, and he may struggle with communicating in a way that doesn't come across as cold or distant.

To overcome these challenges, the Sigma Male can work on developing his emotional intelligence and empathy. This means learning how to recognize and understand his own emotions and the emotions of others, and using this knowledge to communicate more effectively.

One way to do this is to practice active listening. The Sigma Male can make a conscious effort to listen to his partner without interrupting or judging. He can also ask open-ended questions that encourage his partner to share more about their thoughts and feelings.

Another important aspect of communicating as a Sigma Male is knowing when to speak up and when to stay silent. The Sigma Male is not one to engage in meaningless small talk or gossip, but he also knows when it's important to share his opinions and insights.

In a relationship, the Sigma Male may struggle with finding the right balance between being independent and maintaining a connection with his partner. He may need to communicate his need for space or alone time, while also making an effort to stay connected and engaged.

One way to do this is to establish clear boundaries and expectations with his partner. The Sigma Male can communicate his needs and desires in a respectful and assertive manner, while also being open to compromise and negotiation.

Finally, communicating as a Sigma Male requires a level of self-awareness and self-confidence. The Sigma Male knows who he is and what he wants, and he is not afraid to assert himself in a relationship. He communicates with purpose and intention, and he expects the same from his partner.

In conclusion, communicating as a Sigma Male is all about being honest, direct, and authentic. The Sigma Male values transparency and integrity, and he expects the same from those around him. By developing his emotional intelligence and empathy, establishing clear boundaries and expectations, and communicating with purpose and intention, the Sigma Male can build strong and fulfilling relationships with those around him.

3.3 The Sigma Male's Approach to Intimacy

Intimacy is an essential aspect of any healthy relationship. It is the glue that binds two people together and allows them to feel a deep emotional connection. For a Sigma male, the approach to intimacy may be different from that of other men. In this chapter, we will explore the Sigma male's approach to intimacy and how it affects his relationships.

The Sigma male is an independent man who values his freedom and autonomy. He is not interested in conforming to societal norms or following the crowd. Instead, he prefers to forge his own path and live life on his own terms. This independent streak also extends to his approach to intimacy. Unlike other men who may be more traditional in their approach to relationships, the Sigma male takes a more unconventional approach to intimacy.

At the core of the Sigma male's approach to intimacy is the belief that it should be a conscious choice. He is not interested in superficial connections or casual flings. Instead, he seeks out deeper and more meaningful relationships that are built on a foundation of mutual respect and understanding. For the Sigma male, intimacy is not something that should be rushed into or taken lightly. It is a process that requires time, patience, and a willingness to be vulnerable.

One of the key differences between the Sigma male and other men when it comes to intimacy is his ability to communicate his needs and desires. He is not afraid to express his emotions and share his deepest thoughts with his partner. This level of openness and honesty is rare in today's society, where many men are taught to be stoic and unemotional. For the Sigma male, however, communication is essential for building trust and intimacy in a relationship.

Another important aspect of the Sigma male's approach to intimacy is his ability to respect his partner's boundaries. He understands that everyone has their own unique needs and desires when it comes to intimacy, and he is willing to adapt to his partner's preferences. Whether it's taking things slow or exploring new experiences, the Sigma male is always willing to listen and adjust his approach accordingly.

Perhaps the most significant difference between the Sigma male and other men when it comes to intimacy is his ability to maintain his independence within a relationship. Unlike other men who may become codependent on their partners, the Sigma male values his freedom and autonomy. He understands that a healthy relationship is one where both partners are independent and self-sufficient. This allows him to pursue his own interests and goals while still maintaining a deep emotional connection with his partner.

Of course, this approach to intimacy is not without its challenges. The Sigma male's unconventional approach may be perceived as aloof or distant by some partners. His focus on independence and autonomy may also be difficult for some to reconcile with the traditional roles of men in relationships. However, for those who are willing to embrace the Sigma male's approach, it can lead to a deeper and more fulfilling connection.

In conclusion, the Sigma male's approach to intimacy is one that prioritizes choice, communication, respect, and independence. He is not interested in superficial connections or casual flings, but instead seeks out deeper and more meaningful relationships. By communicating his needs and desires, respecting his partner's boundaries, and maintaining his independence within a relationship, the Sigma male is able to build strong and lasting connections with his partners. While this approach may not be for everyone, for those who are willing to embrace it, it can lead to a fulfilling and rewarding relationship.

3.4 Managing Expectations in Relationships

One of the key challenges for the Sigma Male in relationships is managing expectations. This is because the Sigma Male is often independent and prefers to do things on his own terms. This can create friction in relationships, especially if the other partner has different expectations.

To manage expectations effectively, the Sigma Male needs to communicate clearly and honestly with his partner. This means being upfront about his needs, desires, and limitations. It also means being willing to compromise and to listen to his partner's needs.

One of the biggest challenges for the Sigma Male is to balance his independence with his commitment to the relationship. This can be difficult, as the Sigma Male may be used to making his own decisions and may not be comfortable sharing control with his partner.

To overcome this challenge, the Sigma Male needs to be willing to share responsibility and to work collaboratively with his partner. This can involve compromise, negotiation, and a willingness to put the needs of the relationship ahead of his own desires.

Another important aspect of managing expectations in relationships is setting boundaries. The Sigma Male may be used to having a lot of personal space and time, but this can create problems in relationships if his partner feels neglected or ignored.

To set boundaries, the Sigma Male needs to communicate his needs clearly and assertively. He also needs to be willing to respect his partner's boundaries and to compromise when necessary.

Finally, managing expectations in relationships requires patience and understanding. The Sigma Male may be used to being independent, but in a relationship, he needs to be willing to adapt and to learn from his partner.

This may involve making adjustments to his lifestyle, his communication style, or his habits. It may also involve being patient and understanding when his partner has different expectations or needs.

In conclusion, managing expectations is a key challenge for the Sigma Male in relationships. However, with clear communication, compromise, and a willingness to adapt, the Sigma Male can create successful and fulfilling relationships.

3.5 Balancing Ambition and Relationships

The Sigma Male is often regarded as the epitome of independence and self-sufficiency. These men are driven, ambitious, and fiercely focused on achieving their goals. They are not afraid to take risks or challenge the status quo in pursuit of what they want. However, this intense focus on personal success can sometimes come at the cost of their relationships.

Balancing ambition and relationships is a delicate dance that many Sigma Males struggle to master. On one hand, they are driven to achieve greatness and make a name for themselves. On the other hand, they crave connection and intimacy with others. Finding a way to strike a balance between these two competing desires can be a challenge.

One of the main reasons Sigma Males struggle with balancing ambition and relationships is that they often have very high standards for themselves and others. They expect excellence in all areas of their life, and they want their partners to be equally driven and successful. This can create a dynamic where work and achievement take priority over relationships and personal connections.

Moreover, Sigma Males tend to be fiercely independent and self-sufficient. They are used to relying on themselves and may not be comfortable relying on others for emotional support. This can make it challenging to form deep and meaningful relationships, as they may struggle to open up and share their innermost thoughts and feelings with others.

To successfully balance ambition and relationships, Sigma Males need to cultivate a few key skills and behaviors.

First and foremost, they need to learn to prioritize their relationships alongside their goals. This means making time for their partners, even when they are busy or stressed at work. It may mean saying no to certain opportunities or obligations to ensure that they are investing enough time and energy into their personal connections.

Secondly, Sigma Males need to work on their communication skills. They need to learn how to express their feelings and needs in a clear and direct way. This includes learning to ask for help when they need it and being willing to accept support from others.

Thirdly, Sigma Males need to practice vulnerability. This can be a challenging task for independent and self-sufficient individuals, but it is essential for forming deep and meaningful connections with others. Vulnerability requires being willing to share one's fears, flaws, and weaknesses with others. It means accepting that it is okay to not have everything under control all the time and that it is okay to need help and support from others.

Finally, Sigma Males need to learn to set boundaries. They need to understand that it is okay to say no to certain opportunities or obligations if they are going to interfere with their personal relationships. They also need to learn how to communicate their boundaries in a clear and direct way, so that others understand their needs and can respect them.

Balancing ambition and relationships is not an easy task, but it is essential for Sigma Males who want to lead fulfilling and successful lives. By prioritizing their personal connections and investing in their communication skills, vulnerability, and boundary-setting abilities, Sigma Males can find a way to achieve their goals while also maintaining meaningful and fulfilling relationships with those around them.

3.6 Dealing with Conflict as a Sigma Male

Conflict is inevitable in any relationship, and the Sigma male is no stranger to it. As someone who values independence and autonomy, the Sigma male may find it challenging to navigate conflict in relationships. However, with the right mindset and approach, he can effectively deal with conflict and maintain healthy relationships.

One of the first steps in dealing with conflict as a Sigma male is to understand the source of the conflict. Many conflicts arise from a difference in values or goals, so it is important to identify what is causing the disagreement. Once the source of the conflict is identified, the Sigma male can take steps to address it directly and find a solution that works for both parties.

It is also important for the Sigma male to approach conflict with a calm and rational mindset. As someone who values independence and autonomy, it can be easy to become defensive or dismissive when faced with conflict. However, this can only escalate the situation and make it more difficult to find a resolution. Instead, the Sigma male should take a step back, assess the situation, and approach the conflict with an open mind and a willingness to listen to the other person's perspective.

Communication is key when dealing with conflict, and the Sigma male should strive to communicate clearly and effectively. This means being honest and direct about his feelings and needs, while also being willing to listen to the other person's point of view. It is important to avoid using accusatory language or making assumptions about the other person's intentions. Instead, the Sigma male should focus on expressing his own needs and working with the other person to find a solution that works for both parties.

Another important aspect of dealing with conflict as a Sigma male is to maintain boundaries and assertiveness. As someone who values independence and autonomy, it can be tempting to give in to the other person's demands or compromise too much in order to avoid conflict. However, this can lead to resentment and frustration over time. Instead, the Sigma male should be willing to stand up for his own needs and boundaries, while also being willing to compromise and find a solution that works for both parties.

Finally, it is important for the Sigma male to be willing to take a break or step away from the situation if necessary. Conflict can be emotionally taxing, and it is important to take care of oneself in the midst of a disagreement. This may mean taking a break to cool down or seeking support from friends or family members. By taking care of oneself, the Sigma male can approach the conflict with a clearer and more rational mind, which can lead to a more effective resolution.

In conclusion, conflict is inevitable in any relationship, but it is possible for the Sigma male to effectively deal with it and maintain healthy relationships. By identifying the source of the conflict, approaching it with a calm and rational mindset, communicating effectively, maintaining boundaries and assertiveness, and taking care of oneself, the Sigma male can navigate conflict in a way that supports his values of independence and autonomy while also fostering healthy relationships with others.

3.7 The Benefits of Being a Sigma Male in a Relationship

As a Sigma Male, being in a relationship can be a unique experience. While society may view relationships as a means to settle down and conform, Sigma Males approach them from a different perspective. They value independence, self-reliance, and nonconformity. These traits make them excellent partners, and there are many benefits to being a Sigma Male in a relationship.

One of the most significant benefits of being a Sigma Male in a relationship is the freedom that it allows. Sigma Males are not interested in controlling their partners or being controlled themselves. They value independence, and they respect their partner's independence as well. This means that in a relationship, both partners can pursue their own interests and passions without feeling stifled or limited.

In addition, Sigma Males are not interested in playing games or engaging in drama. They are honest and straightforward, which means that their partners can trust them completely. This trust is essential in any relationship, and it allows both partners to feel secure and confident in their connection.

Sigma Males are also excellent problem solvers. They are independent thinkers who approach challenges with creativity and resourcefulness. This means that in a relationship, they can be relied upon to find solutions to any issue that arises. They don't shy away from difficult conversations or situations, and they are not afraid to be vulnerable with their partners. This openness and honesty create a deep and meaningful connection between partners.

Another benefit of being a Sigma Male in a relationship is the ability to maintain boundaries. Sigma Males are not interested in sacrificing their personal space or time for the sake of a relationship. They value their independence and their alone time, and they are not willing to compromise on these things. This means that their partners must respect their boundaries, which can create a healthy and balanced relationship.

Sigma Males are also not interested in conforming to societal norms or expectations. They are independent thinkers who forge their paths in life. This means that they are not interested in traditional gender roles or stereotypes. They are happy to share responsibilities and chores with their partners, and they do not view any task as strictly "masculine" or "feminine." This fluidity can create a more egalitarian and balanced relationship where both partners feel valued and respected.

Another benefit of being a Sigma Male in a relationship is the ability to prioritize personal growth and development. Sigma Males are always striving to improve themselves and their lives. They are not interested in becoming complacent or stagnant. This means that in a relationship, they will encourage their partners to pursue their passions and goals. They will support their partner's personal growth and development, and they will not hold them back. This creates a dynamic and fulfilling relationship where both partners can thrive and grow.

Sigma Males are also not interested in superficial connections or relationships based on appearances. They value substance and meaningful connections. This means that in a relationship, they will prioritize emotional intimacy and connection over physical attraction or material possessions. They will create a deep and meaningful connection with their partner based on mutual respect, honesty, and trust.

Finally, being a Sigma Male in a relationship means having the freedom to express oneself fully. Sigma Males are independent thinkers who are not afraid to be themselves. This means that in a relationship, they will express their emotions and feelings freely. They will not hold back or pretend to be someone they are not. This creates an honest and authentic relationship where both partners can be themselves fully.

In conclusion, being a Sigma Male in a relationship can be a unique and fulfilling experience. Sigma Males value independence, nonconformity, and personal growth. These traits make them excellent partners, and there are many benefits to being in a relationship with a Sigma Male. These benefits include freedom, honesty, problem-solving abilities, boundary maintenance, egalitarianism, personal growth, and meaningful connections. If you are a Sigma Male looking for a fulfilling relationship, embrace your independence and seek a partner who values your unique perspective and traits.

3.8 Understanding the Limitations of Relationships for Sigma Males

The Sigma Male in Relationships

Understanding the Limitations of Relationships for Sigma Males

A Sigma Male is someone who marches to the beat of his own drum. He is independent and self-sufficient, preferring to work alone rather than in a group. He values his freedom and autonomy and dislikes being controlled by others. While Sigma Males can be in relationships, they often struggle to maintain them due to their unique personality traits.

One of the limitations of relationships for Sigma Males is their need for solitude. Unlike an Alpha Male who thrives in social situations, a Sigma Male is comfortable being alone. He needs time to recharge and reflect on his thoughts and emotions. This can be difficult for his partner to understand and accept, especially if they are more outgoing and social. The constant need for space can cause strain and tension in the relationship.

Another limitation for Sigma Males in relationships is their tendency to be non-committal. Sigma Males are fiercely independent and value their freedom. They may be hesitant to commit to a long-term relationship because it requires them to sacrifice their autonomy. This can be frustrating for their partner, who may feel that the relationship is not progressing or that the Sigma Male is not fully invested in the relationship.

Sigma Males value their privacy and can be guarded with their emotions. They may struggle to express their feelings or share details about their personal life with their partner. This can create a distance between them, making it difficult for their partner to connect with them on an emotional level. The lack of emotional intimacy can make it challenging to build a deep and meaningful relationship.

In addition, Sigma Males tend to have a small circle of friends and acquaintances. They value quality over quantity and prefer to have a small group of close and trusted friends. This can make it challenging for their partner to integrate into their social circle. Sigma Males may be reluctant to introduce their partner to their friends, believing that it will disrupt the dynamic or that their partner will not fit in.

Finally, Sigma Males can be stubborn and inflexible. They have a strong sense of self and values and may be resistant to compromise or change. This can create tension in the relationship, as their partner may feel that they are not willing to adapt or compromise to meet their needs. The lack of flexibility can make it challenging to find common ground and make the relationship work.

Despite these limitations, Sigma Males can have successful relationships if they are willing to work on their communication and compromise. They can learn to balance their need for solitude with their partner's need for companionship, and find ways to express their emotions and build emotional intimacy. They can also learn to be more flexible and open-minded, and work on integrating their partner into their social circle.

In conclusion, Sigma Males have unique personality traits that can make it challenging for them to maintain relationships. Their need for solitude, non-committal nature, guarded emotions, small social circle, and inflexibility can create tension and strain in the relationship. However, with work and dedication, Sigma Males can have successful relationships and build deep and meaningful connections with their partners.

3.9 Connecting with Other Sigma Males in Relationships.

Connecting with Other Sigma Males in Relationships

Sigma males are often seen as independent and solitary individuals, but that does not mean they are entirely detached from forming relationships with people. In fact, sigma males can often have deep and meaningful connections with others, but they tend to be more selective in who they choose to involve in their lives. When it comes to connecting with other sigma males in relationships, there are a few things that are important to keep in mind.

The first thing to note is that sigma males tend to be more introspective and focused on their own goals and interests, which can make it challenging to form connections with others. However, when they do make a connection, it tends to be a deeper and more meaningful one than with others. This is because sigma males are selective about who they allow into their lives, and they value quality over quantity when it comes to relationships. This means that if you want to connect with a sigma male, you need to show that you are genuine and have something of value to offer.

One way to connect with other sigma males is through shared interests or hobbies. Sigma males tend to be passionate about their interests and are often very knowledgeable about them. If you share a similar interest or hobby, it can be a great way to connect with a sigma male. Whether it's a shared love of music, film, or a particular sport, finding common ground can help build a connection and open up the possibility of a relationship.

Another way to connect with sigma males is through intellectual conversations. Sigma males tend to be deep thinkers and are often interested in exploring ideas and concepts in-depth. If you can engage them in a meaningful conversation about a topic that interests them, they are more likely to open up and share their thoughts and ideas with you. This can be a great way to build a connection with a sigma male and establish a deeper level of understanding.

When it comes to romantic relationships, sigma males tend to be more cautious and selective in their approach. They are not interested in shallow or superficial connections, and they value emotional depth and authenticity. If you want to connect with a sigma male romantically, you need to show that you are genuine, trustworthy, and have something of value to offer.

One way to do this is to be upfront and honest about your intentions. Sigma males value honesty and authenticity, and they appreciate it when others are direct and straightforward with them. This means being clear about what you are looking for in a relationship and what you have to offer.

Another way to connect with a sigma male romantically is to be patient and understanding. Sigma males tend to take their time when it comes to relationships, and they may need more space and independence than other types of men. It's important to respect their boundaries and give them the time and space they need to feel comfortable and secure in the relationship.

Finally, it's important to understand that sigma males may have a different approach to relationships than other types of men. They may not be as outwardly affectionate or expressive, but that doesn't mean they don't care deeply about their partners. Sigma males tend to show their love and affection in more subtle ways, such as through acts of service or thoughtful gestures.

In conclusion, connecting with other sigma males in relationships can be challenging, but it is possible. It's important to show that you are genuine, authentic, and have something of value to offer. Whether it's through shared interests, intellectual conversations, or a romantic connection, building a relationship with a sigma male takes time and patience. But if you are willing to put in the effort, the rewards can be deep and meaningful connections that last a lifetime.

4. Navigating the Workplace as a Sigma Male

4.1 The Challenge of Corporate Culture

For many Sigma males, navigating the workplace can be a challenge. This is particularly true when it comes to the corporate culture of large organizations. Corporate culture refers to the shared values, beliefs, norms, and behaviors that characterize an organization. It is often seen as the glue that holds an organization together and shapes how employees behave and interact with one another. However, for Sigma males, corporate culture can often feel stifling and limiting.

One of the challenges Sigma males face when it comes to corporate culture is the pressure to conform. Corporate cultures often prioritize conformity and compliance over individuality and creativity. They can be rigid and hierarchical, with strict rules and expectations for how employees should dress, behave, and communicate. This can be particularly challenging for Sigma males, who value independence and autonomy and may chafe at the idea of being told what to do or how to act.

Another challenge Sigma males face in corporate culture is the emphasis on teamwork and collaboration. While these values can be beneficial for organizations, they can also be challenging for Sigma males, who often prefer to work independently and may struggle with group dynamics. Additionally, corporate cultures can often promote a sense of competition among employees, which can be difficult for Sigma males who prefer to focus on their own work rather than engaging in office politics or trying to outdo their colleagues.

The emphasis on conformity and teamwork in corporate culture can also make it difficult for Sigma males to express their creativity and individuality. Corporate cultures often prioritize efficiency and productivity over innovation and risk-taking, which can stifle the creativity and independent thinking of Sigma males. Additionally, the pressure to conform can make it challenging for Sigma males to stand out or make their mark in the organization.

Despite these challenges, Sigma males can still thrive in corporate culture by leveraging their unique strengths and characteristics. For example, Sigma males often excel at critical thinking, problem-solving, and independent work, which can be valuable assets in many organizations. Additionally, Sigma males can use their natural ability to observe and analyze their environment to gain a deeper understanding of the corporate culture and identify opportunities to navigate it more effectively.

One strategy Sigma males can use to navigate corporate culture is to focus on building strong relationships with their colleagues and superiors. While Sigma males may prefer to work independently, building strong relationships with others can help them navigate the politics and dynamics of the organization. Additionally, by building strong relationships, Sigma males can gain allies and advocates who can help them advance their goals and ideas within the organization.

Another strategy Sigma males can use is to focus on developing their communication and collaboration skills. While Sigma males may prefer to work independently, developing their ability to communicate effectively and work collaboratively can help them navigate the teamwork and collaboration-focused culture of many organizations. Additionally, by developing these skills, Sigma males can better express their ideas and perspectives to others and build stronger relationships with their colleagues.

Finally, Sigma males can leverage their natural ability to observe and analyze their environment to identify opportunities for growth and advancement within the organization. By staying attuned to the culture and dynamics of the organization, Sigma males can identify where their skills and strengths can be best utilized and where they can have the greatest impact.

In conclusion, navigating corporate culture can be a challenge for Sigma males, who value independence, autonomy, and individuality. However, by leveraging their unique strengths and characteristics and focusing on building strong relationships, developing communication and collaboration skills, and staying attuned to the culture and dynamics of the organization, Sigma males can navigate corporate culture successfully and thrive in the workplace.

4.2 Building Positive Working Relationships

As a Sigma male, you may often find yourself in a position where you need to navigate your way through the workplace with ease. One of the most important aspects of achieving success in any workplace is building positive working relationships with your colleagues and superiors. While this can be a daunting task for some, with a little effort and the right mindset, it is certainly achievable.

One of the key ingredients to building positive working relationships is communication. As a Sigma male, you may not be the most talkative person in the room, but it is important to understand that effective communication is essential in any workplace. This does not mean that you need to become a chatterbox or engage in small talk, but it does mean that you should be clear and concise when you do communicate. You should also be open to feedback and willing to listen to the ideas of others. This will not only help you to build relationships, but it will also help you to develop professionally.

Another important factor in building positive working relationships is respect. You should always treat your colleagues and superiors with respect, regardless of their position or status within the company. This means being polite, courteous, and professional at all times. You should also avoid gossip and negativity, as this can be detrimental to your relationships and your reputation within the workplace.

In addition to communication and respect, another key ingredient in building positive working relationships is trust. You should strive to be reliable and dependable, and always follow through on your commitments. If you say you will do something, make sure you do it. This will help to establish trust with your colleagues and superiors, and will make it easier for you to collaborate and work together on projects.

Another important aspect of building positive working relationships is being a team player. While Sigma males are often independent and self-sufficient, it is important to understand that success in the workplace often requires teamwork. You should be willing to collaborate with others and be open to new ideas and perspectives. This will not only help you to build relationships, but it will also help you to achieve your goals more effectively.

Finally, it is important to be proactive in building positive working relationships. This means reaching out to your colleagues and superiors, and taking the initiative to build connections and establish rapport. This can be as simple as scheduling a coffee or lunch meeting, or volunteering to help out with a project. By taking the initiative, you will demonstrate your commitment to the job and your willingness to work with others.

In conclusion, building positive working relationships is essential for success in any workplace, and it is particularly important for Sigma males who may struggle with social interactions. By focusing on communication, respect, trust, teamwork, and proactivity, you can establish positive relationships with your colleagues and superiors, and achieve your goals more effectively.

4.3 Playing the Game: Navigating Office Politics

The Sigma Male is a unique individual in the workplace due to their independent nature and tendency to avoid traditional hierarchies. However, navigating office politics is an essential skill for any professional, and the Sigma Male can benefit from understanding how to play the game without compromising their values or independence.

Firstly, it is crucial to recognize that office politics is an inevitable part of any workplace, no matter how small or large the organization. It is human nature to form alliances and compete for positions of power and influence. The Sigma Male needs to acknowledge this and be prepared to engage in politics to a certain extent.

However, the Sigma Male also needs to be aware of the potential pitfalls of office politics, such as favoritism, gossiping, and backstabbing. Instead of getting caught up in these negative aspects, the Sigma Male should focus on building positive relationships with colleagues, based on mutual respect and trust.

One way to achieve this is by being authentic and genuine in all interactions with others in the workplace. The Sigma Male should avoid pretending to be someone they are not, as this can come across as insincere and ultimately damage their reputation. Instead, they should be true to themselves while also being respectful of others' opinions and perspectives.

Another important aspect of navigating office politics is understanding who wields power in the workplace and how they operate. The Sigma Male should take the time to observe how decisions are made, who has influence, and what drives these individuals. By gaining this insight, the Sigma Male can better position themselves to build alliances and influence decision-making.

However, it is important to note that the Sigma Male should not compromise their values or integrity to gain favor with those in power. Instead, they should focus on building relationships based on shared goals and values, while also being willing to respectfully challenge any decisions or actions that go against these principles.

In addition to building relationships with colleagues, the Sigma Male should also focus on building their personal brand and reputation within the workplace. This can be achieved by delivering high-quality work, being reliable and dependable, and demonstrating a willingness to go above and beyond in their role.

Furthermore, the Sigma Male should be proactive in seeking out opportunities to showcase their skills and expertise. This can be done by volunteering for projects or initiatives that align with their interests and strengths, as well as networking with colleagues and industry peers.

Finally, the Sigma Male should also be aware that office politics can be influenced by external factors, such as economic conditions, industry trends, and changes in leadership. Therefore, it is essential to stay up-to-date on these developments and adapt their approach accordingly.

In summary, navigating office politics is an essential skill for any professional, including the Sigma Male. By being authentic, building positive relationships, understanding power dynamics, maintaining their values and integrity, building their personal brand, being proactive, and adapting to external factors, the Sigma Male can successfully navigate office politics while remaining true to their independent nature.

4.4 The Importance of Assertiveness

Assertiveness is a crucial skill for any individual, but especially for a Sigma Male navigating the workplace. Assertiveness is the ability to express oneself in a confident and clear manner, without being aggressive or passive. Assertiveness involves setting boundaries, being able to say no, and communicating effectively with colleagues, superiors, and subordinates.

Being assertive in the workplace is essential for several reasons. Firstly, it allows a Sigma Male to establish boundaries and maintain personal and professional integrity. It is important for a Sigma Male to be able to say no to requests that go against their values or interests, without fear of reprisal. By being assertive, a Sigma Male can communicate their needs and expectations effectively and maintain their autonomy.

Secondly, assertiveness is essential for effective communication. Being able to express oneself clearly and confidently can help a Sigma Male to avoid misunderstandings and conflicts. It allows them to communicate their ideas and opinions effectively, and to provide feedback to colleagues and superiors in a constructive manner.

Thirdly, being assertive can help a Sigma Male to advance in their career. Being confident and clear in communication can help them to stand out in a crowded workplace. It shows colleagues and superiors that they are confident in their abilities and willing to take on new challenges. It can lead to opportunities for promotion and increased responsibility.

However, it is important to note that assertiveness should not be confused with aggression. Aggression involves expressing oneself in a forceful and confrontational manner, often at the expense of others. Aggressive behavior can damage relationships with colleagues and superiors, and can lead to a negative reputation in the workplace.

Assertiveness, on the other hand, involves expressing oneself in a confident and clear manner, while respecting the needs and opinions of others. It involves listening to others and being open to feedback, while also communicating one's own needs and expectations.

Developing assertiveness as a Sigma Male requires practice and self-reflection. It involves identifying one's own values and priorities, and communicating them effectively to others. It also involves developing strong interpersonal skills, such as active listening and empathy. By developing assertiveness, a Sigma Male can navigate the workplace with confidence and integrity, and achieve their goals and aspirations.

4.5 Managing Stress in the Workplace

In today's fast-paced work environment, it can be challenging for people to manage stress. Working long hours, juggling multiple projects, meeting deadlines, and dealing with difficult colleagues can all create stress that can take a toll on one's mental and physical health. As a Sigma Male, managing stress in the workplace is crucial to maintaining your independence and success. Here are some tips to help you navigate the workplace while keeping your stress levels in check.

1. Set Boundaries

Setting boundaries is one of the most important things you can do to manage stress in the workplace. As a Sigma Male, you value your independence and autonomy, and you may be hesitant to speak up for yourself. However, setting boundaries is essential to preserving your mental and physical wellbeing. Communicate your needs clearly to your colleagues and superiors, and don't be afraid to say no if you feel overwhelmed or overworked. This can help you avoid burnout and maintain a work-life balance that works for you.

2. Practice Mindfulness

Mindfulness is a powerful tool for managing stress in the workplace. By focusing on the present moment and becoming aware of your thoughts and feelings, you can reduce stress and increase your ability to handle challenges. Try to incorporate mindfulness into your daily routine, whether it's through meditation, deep breathing, or simply taking a few moments to clear your mind. This can help you stay calm and focused in the midst of a busy workday.

3. Take Breaks

Taking breaks throughout the day is important for managing stress and staying productive. Even a short break can help you recharge your batteries and reduce tension. Whether it's a walk outside, a quick stretch, or a chat with a colleague, taking breaks can help you stay energized and engaged throughout the day. Additionally, make sure to take longer breaks when necessary, such as taking a vacation or a mental health day. This can help you avoid burnout and maintain your independence over the long term.

4. Practice Assertiveness

As a Sigma Male, you may find it challenging to assert yourself in the workplace. However, practicing assertiveness can help you manage stress and maintain your independence. Assertiveness means speaking up for yourself and expressing your needs and opinions clearly and respectfully. This can help you avoid conflict, build healthy relationships with colleagues and superiors, and avoid being taken advantage of. It can also help you maintain your autonomy and independence in the workplace.

5. Seek Support

Finally, it's important to seek support when you're feeling stressed in the workplace. Whether it's talking to a trusted colleague, seeking advice from a mentor, or seeking professional help from a therapist, seeking support can help you manage stress and stay on track. As a Sigma Male, you may be hesitant to ask for help, but remember that asking for help is a sign of strength, not weakness. It can help you maintain your independence and resilience over the long term.

In conclusion, managing stress in the workplace is crucial to maintaining your independence and success as a Sigma Male. By setting boundaries, practicing mindfulness, taking breaks, practicing assertiveness, and seeking support, you can navigate the workplace with confidence and ease. Remember that managing stress is an ongoing process, and it's important to prioritize your mental and physical wellbeing as you navigate your career. With these tips, you can stay on track and achieve your goals while maintaining your autonomy and independence.

4.6 The Sigma Male's Unique Approach to Leadership

Leadership is a trait that is often associated with the alpha male, the individual who is dominant, assertive, and authoritative. However, a sigma male's unique approach to leadership presents a valuable perspective on the subject. Sigma males are known for their independence, self-reliance, and non-conformity. As a result, they tend to have a distinct approach to leadership that is grounded in their values, principles, and individuality.

The first and perhaps most significant characteristic of the sigma male's leadership style is their ability to forge their path. Unlike alpha males who tend to follow a predetermined set of rules or societal norms, sigma males are more likely to chart their course. They are not afraid to take risks, make unconventional decisions, or challenge the status quo. This trait is particularly crucial in leadership positions where the conventional approach may not be suitable, and innovation is required. Sigma males can bring a new perspective to a problem and develop solutions that others may not have considered.

Another essential aspect of the sigma male's leadership style is their ability to be self-reliant. Sigma males are not dependent on anyone else to achieve their goals. They have a strong sense of individualism and are comfortable working alone, which makes them effective in leadership positions where autonomy is necessary. Sigma males can make decisions independently, and they do not require the approval of others to move forward. This quality can help them navigate challenging situations and make difficult decisions with ease.

In addition to being self-reliant, sigma males are good at building relationships. Even though they prefer working independently, sigma males understand the importance of collaboration and teamwork. They are good at working with people who share their values and principles, and they are not afraid to delegate tasks to others. Sigma males recognize that everyone has unique strengths that can be utilized, and by working together, they can achieve more significant results. They understand the importance of building trust, respect, and loyalty, and they work hard to develop and maintain healthy relationships with their team members.

Another aspect of the sigma male's leadership style is their ability to lead by example. Sigma males are not interested in telling people what to do; they prefer to show them. They lead through their actions, and their words match their deeds. Sigma males understand that they cannot demand respect; they have to earn it. By leading by example, sigma males can inspire others to follow their lead and achieve their goals.

Sigma males are also excellent problem-solvers. They have a unique perspective on the world, and they tend to think outside the box. Sigma males are not afraid to challenge traditional assumptions, and they can identify problems that others may overlook. They are skilled at analyzing complex issues and developing practical solutions that are both effective and efficient. Sigma males are good at breaking down problems into smaller, more manageable parts, and they can identify the root cause of an issue quickly.

Finally, sigma males are adaptable. They are not afraid of change and are comfortable in new and challenging situations. Sigma males understand that change is inevitable, and they are ready to embrace it. They are not afraid to try new things, and they are open to new ideas and perspectives. This trait is particularly valuable in leadership positions where the ability to adapt to changing environments is crucial.

In conclusion, the sigma male's unique approach to leadership presents a valuable perspective on the subject. Sigma males are not afraid to chart their course, and they are comfortable working independently. They understand the importance of collaboration and teamwork, and they are good at building relationships. Sigma males lead by example, are excellent problem-solvers, and are adaptable to changing situations. These traits make them effective leaders who can navigate the workplace with ease.

4.7 Balancing Work and Personal Life

One of the biggest challenges that come with being a Sigma male is finding the right balance between work and personal life. Sigma males are often driven and ambitious, and they put in long hours to achieve their goals. However, this can come at the cost of neglecting personal relationships and other aspects of their lives. In this section, we will explore some tips and strategies for Sigma males to balance their work and personal life.

Set Boundaries

The first step in achieving a work-life balance is to set clear boundaries. This means deciding on the amount of time and energy you want to dedicate to work and personal life. Sigma males often find it challenging to separate work from personal life because they are so invested in their work. However, it is crucial to set boundaries and stick to them to avoid burnout and maintain healthy relationships.

One effective way to set boundaries is to establish a fixed schedule for work and personal activities. For example, scheduling a specific time for work and dedicating time outside of work to hobbies, self-care, and spending time with loved ones. Setting boundaries also means learning to say no to work requests that conflict with personal time. It may be challenging, but it is essential to communicate your needs and priorities to your colleagues and employers.

Prioritize Self-Care

Self-care is a critical component of achieving a work-life balance. Sigma males tend to be so focused on achieving their goals that they forget to take care of themselves. Prioritizing self-care means taking time to relax, exercise, eat healthily, and get enough sleep. These activities can help to reduce stress and improve overall well-being.

Sigma males can incorporate self-care activities into their daily routine by scheduling time for exercise, meditation, or taking a break when needed. It is essential to recognize that self-care is not a luxury but a necessity for a healthy work-life balance. Taking care of yourself allows you to be more productive, focused, and energized at work and enhances your personal relationships.

Maintain Healthy Relationships

Maintaining healthy relationships is a crucial aspect of work-life balance. Sigma males often find it challenging to balance work and relationships because they prioritize work over personal life. However, neglecting personal relationships can take a toll on mental health and overall well-being. To maintain healthy relationships, Sigma males need to invest time and effort in building and nurturing relationships.

One way to maintain healthy relationships is to communicate effectively with loved ones. Communication is vital in any relationship, and Sigma males need to communicate their needs and expectations clearly. It is also important to make time for loved ones by scheduling regular activities and events.

Another way to maintain healthy relationships is to set boundaries with work. Sigma males need to communicate their work schedule and availability to loved ones to avoid conflicts. They can also incorporate loved ones into their work by sharing their successes and challenges with them.

Take Time off

Taking time off work is essential for achieving a work-life balance. Sigma males tend to be workaholics, and taking time off can feel like a sign of weakness. However, taking time off work is crucial for mental health, physical health, and overall well-being. It is essential to take time off work to recharge, relax, and enjoy personal activities.

Sigma males can take time off work by planning vacations, staycations, or personal retreats. It is important to disconnect from work during this time and focus on personal activities. Taking time off work also means learning to delegate tasks and responsibilities to colleagues and employees.

Conclusion

Achieving a work-life balance is a challenge for Sigma males, but it is not impossible. Setting boundaries, prioritizing self-care, maintaining healthy relationships, and taking time off work are essential components of a healthy work-life balance. Sigma males need to remember that work is not everything, and personal relationships and activities are equally important for mental and physical health. By prioritizing work and personal life, Sigma males can achieve a healthy work-life balance and live a fulfilling life.

4.8 Finding Fulfillment in Your Career

In today's world, finding fulfillment in your career can be a difficult task, especially for sigma males. Sigma males are independent, non-conforming, and often go against the norm. They don't seek validation from others and tend to be fiercely individualistic. This can make it challenging for them to fit into traditional career paths and find fulfillment in their work.

However, with the right mindset and approach, sigma males can find fulfillment in their careers. Here are some tips on how to do so:

1. Define Your Own Success

Sigma males do not conform to society's expectations for success. They define their own success and what it means to them. This means that they need to have a clear understanding of what they want to achieve in their career.

To find fulfillment in your career, you need to know what success means to you. It could be financial stability, career growth, making a positive impact, or a combination of these. Once you know what success means to you, you can set goals and work towards achieving them.

2. Follow Your Passion

Sigma males are passionate about what they do. They don't settle for a job that pays the bills but doesn't fulfill them. They pursue their passions and find ways to turn them into a career.

To find fulfillment in your career, you need to follow your passion. This means identifying what you love to do and finding ways to incorporate it into your work. It could be starting your own business, working for a company that aligns with your values, or pursuing a career in a field you love.

3. Embrace Your Uniqueness

Sigma males are unique individuals who don't conform to the norm. They have their own way of thinking and doing things. This uniqueness can be a strength in the workplace.

To find fulfillment in your career, you need to embrace your uniqueness. This means not trying to fit into a mold that doesn't suit you. Instead, you should focus on your strengths and find ways to use them in your work. This could mean taking on projects that allow you to showcase your unique skills or finding a job that values your individuality.

4. Take Risks

Sigma males are not afraid to take risks. They are willing to step out of their comfort zone and try new things. This can be a valuable trait in the workplace.

To find fulfillment in your career, you need to take risks: This means being open to new opportunities, even if they are outside of your comfort zone. It could mean taking on a project that you've never done before, moving to a new city for a job, or starting your own business. Taking risks can lead to growth and new opportunities.

5. Network

Sigma males may be independent, but they still need to network. Building relationships with others in your industry can lead to new opportunities and connections.

To find fulfillment in your career, you need to network. This means attending industry events, joining professional organizations, and connecting with others in your field. Networking can lead to new job opportunities, collaborations, and mentorship.

6. Find Work-Life Balance

Sigma males are often passionate about their work, but they also need to find balance in their lives. Work-life balance is essential for mental health and overall well-being.

To find fulfillment in your career, you need to find work-life balance. This means setting boundaries and prioritizing self-care. It could mean taking breaks throughout the day, setting aside time for hobbies and interests, or finding ways to disconnect from work when you're off the clock.

In conclusion, finding fulfillment in your career as a sigma male requires a unique approach. It means defining your own success, following your passion, embracing your uniqueness, taking risks, networking, and finding work-life balance. By incorporating these strategies into your career, you can find fulfillment and success on your own terms.

4.9 Dealing with Burnout and Job Dissatisfaction

One of the biggest challenges Sigma males face in the workplace is burnout and job dissatisfaction. This is especially true for those who are highly skilled and motivated, as they tend to take on more responsibility and work longer hours than their peers. As a result, they are often at risk of burning out, which can lead to a decline in job satisfaction, performance, and overall quality of life.

To avoid burnout and job dissatisfaction, Sigma males need to take a proactive approach to managing their workload and maintaining a healthy work-life balance. This requires a combination of self-awareness, boundary setting, and effective time management skills.

Self-Awareness

The first step in avoiding burnout is to develop a strong sense of self-awareness. This means being honest with yourself about your strengths, weaknesses, and limitations, and understanding how they impact your work. For example, if you tend to be a perfectionist, you may need to be aware of how this trait can lead to unrealistic expectations and increased stress. Similarly, if you tend to be a people-pleaser, you may need to be aware of how this trait can lead to over-commitment and a lack of time for yourself.

To develop self-awareness, Sigma males should regularly reflect on their work habits and patterns. This can be done through journaling, meditation, or simply taking time to think about your day. By paying attention to how you feel and what triggers stress, you can begin to identify patterns and develop strategies for managing them.

Boundary Setting

Another important factor in avoiding burnout is boundary setting. This means learning to say no when you need to, and setting clear expectations with your coworkers and boss about your workload and availability. This can be challenging for Sigma males, who may feel pressure to take on more work or to be available to others at all times. However, setting clear boundaries is essential for maintaining a healthy work-life balance and avoiding burnout.

To set boundaries effectively, Sigma males should be clear about their priorities and communicate them with their coworkers and boss. This may mean saying no to certain tasks or projects, or setting specific times when you are not available for work-related calls or emails. By setting boundaries and sticking to them, Sigma males can create a more manageable workload and avoid feeling overwhelmed.

Time Management

Effective time management is another key factor in avoiding burnout and job dissatisfaction. This means learning to prioritize tasks and manage your time effectively, so that you can meet your deadlines without sacrificing your health or personal life. This can be particularly challenging for Sigma males, who may be juggling multiple projects or deadlines at once.

To manage your time effectively, Sigma males should learn to prioritize tasks based on their importance and urgency. This may involve creating a to-do list or using a time management app to keep track of your tasks and deadlines. It may also involve delegating tasks to others or seeking help when needed, rather than trying to do everything yourself.

Conclusion

In conclusion, burnout and job dissatisfaction are common challenges for Sigma males in the workplace. However, by developing self-awareness, setting clear boundaries, and managing their time effectively, Sigma males can avoid burnout and maintain a healthy work-life balance. By taking a proactive approach to managing their workload and prioritizing their well-being, Sigma males can thrive in their careers and achieve their goals.

4.10 The Benefits of Entrepreneurship for Sigma Males.

The world of entrepreneurship has long been associated with the alpha male personality type. However, the truth is that entrepreneurship can be an incredibly rewarding path for sigma males as well. In fact, sigma males possess many qualities that lend themselves well to starting and running a successful business. In this chapter, we will explore the benefits of entrepreneurship for sigma males and how they can navigate the business world to their advantage.

One of the primary benefits of entrepreneurship for sigma males is the ability to control their own destiny. Sigma males value independence and autonomy above all else, and entrepreneurship provides a way to achieve this by being their own boss. The ability to make their own decisions and set their own goals is incredibly appealing to sigma males, who often find the rigid structure of traditional corporate environments stifling. With their natural inclination towards self-reliance, sigma males are well-suited to the unpredictable nature of entrepreneurship, where they must think on their feet and adapt to changing circumstances.

Another benefit of entrepreneurship for sigma males is the opportunity to pursue their passions and interests. Sigma males are often driven by a strong sense of purpose and a desire to make a meaningful impact on the world. Starting their own business allows them to align their work with their values and pursue projects that are truly meaningful to them. This can lead to a greater sense of fulfillment and satisfaction in their work, which in turn can lead to greater success.

Entrepreneurship also allows sigma males to work on their own terms. Sigma males value flexibility and the ability to work in a way that suits their unique strengths and preferences. With their strong independent streak, they are often uncomfortable with the rigid hierarchy and rules of traditional corporate environments. Starting their own business allows them to create a work environment that suits them, from the hours they work to the tasks they focus on. This level of control can be incredibly empowering for sigma males, who often feel out of place in more structured work environments.

Another benefit of entrepreneurship for sigma males is the opportunity to build something from scratch. Sigma males are often creative and innovative, with a natural talent for problem-solving. Starting a business allows them to channel these skills into building something entirely new and unique. This can be incredibly satisfying for sigma males, who enjoy the challenge of turning an idea into a reality. Additionally, the ability to create something from scratch can be a powerful motivator, driving sigma males to work harder and push themselves further than they might in a traditional corporate environment.

Entrepreneurship also offers sigma males the opportunity to build their own brand and reputation. Sigma males are often independent thinkers, with a strong sense of self-reliance. Starting a business allows them to establish themselves as experts in their field and build a reputation for excellence. This can lead to greater recognition and respect from their peers, as well as increased opportunities for growth and expansion. Additionally, by building their own brand, sigma males are not beholden to the reputation of their employer, allowing them to shape their own image and identity in the business world.

While entrepreneurship can be incredibly rewarding for sigma males, it is not without its challenges. Starting a business requires a significant amount of hard work, dedication, and risk-taking. Sigma males may struggle with the uncertainty and unpredictability of entrepreneurship, as well as the need to constantly hustle and promote themselves. Additionally, the isolation of working alone can be challenging for sigma males, who may crave connection and camaraderie with others in the business world.

To navigate the challenges of entrepreneurship, sigma males must leverage their unique strengths and characteristics. They must be willing to take risks and think creatively to solve problems. They must also be comfortable with the uncertainty and unpredictability that comes with starting their own business. Additionally, they must be proactive in seeking out connections and building relationships with others in their industry. By leveraging their strengths and navigating the challenges of entrepreneurship, sigma males can create a successful and fulfilling business that aligns with their values and interests.

In conclusion, entrepreneurship can be an incredibly rewarding path for sigma males. The opportunity to control their own destiny, pursue their passions, and build something from scratch is incredibly appealing to sigma males. However, entrepreneurship is not without its challenges, and sigma males must be willing to take risks and think creatively to succeed. By leveraging their unique strengths and navigating the challenges of entrepreneurship, sigma males can create a successful and fulfilling business that aligns with their values and interests.

5. Embracing Solitude: The Sigma Male's Need for Alone Time

5.1 The Importance of Solitude for Sigma Males

The Sigma Male: Understanding and Navigating the World of the Independent Male is a book that focuses on the unique traits, behaviors, and attitudes of Sigma males. One of the most significant characteristics of Sigma males is their need for solitude. Sigma males are independent, self-sufficient, and prefer to spend time alone rather than in groups or with others. This behavior is not a result of shyness, introversion, or social anxiety. Instead, Sigma males understand the importance of solitude and use it as a tool to enhance their personal growth, creativity, and productivity.

Solitude is critical for Sigma males because it allows them to recharge their mental and emotional batteries. Society is full of distractions, noise, and constant stimulation. With the advent of social media, smartphones, and the internet, it is easy to feel overwhelmed and stressed out. Sigma males recognize this and choose to spend time alone to escape the chaos and noise of the world. This break from the outside world allows them to focus on their thoughts, feelings, and inner desires, which helps them recharge, rejuvenate, and gain clarity.

Another reason why solitude is important for Sigma males is that it allows them to be introspective. Introspection is the act of examining one's thoughts, feelings, and motives. It allows Sigma males to understand themselves better, their values, beliefs, and aspirations. Through introspection, Sigma males can identify their strengths and weaknesses, gain a deeper understanding of their identity, and develop a sense of purpose. This self-reflection is crucial for Sigma males as it enables them to make better decisions, solve complex problems, and achieve their goals.

Solitude also plays a crucial role in enhancing creativity and productivity. Sigma males tend to be creative, innovative, and capable of solving complex problems. However, creativity and productivity require a conducive environment. Solitude provides Sigma males with the space and time needed to access their subconscious mind, where the most creative and innovative ideas reside. When alone, Sigma males can explore their thoughts and ideas without the fear of being judged, criticized, or interrupted. They can let their minds wander, tinker with new concepts, and experiment with new solutions without the pressure of external influences.

Moreover, solitude allows Sigma males to pursue their interests, hobbies, and passions. Sigma males tend to have diverse interests and hobbies that require time, effort, and dedication. They are often engaged in activities that others may not understand or appreciate. Solitude provides Sigma males with the freedom to explore their interests without external distractions or pressures. This freedom allows them to pursue their passions with the dedication, focus, and enthusiasm needed to excel.

Lastly, solitude is essential for Sigma males as it promotes self-reliance and independence. Sigma males value their independence and autonomy. They prefer to rely on themselves rather than on others. Solitude allows them to develop the skills and competencies needed to be self-reliant. When alone, Sigma males learn to rely on themselves for their needs, desires, and aspirations. They become more confident, self-sufficient, and self-aware. This self-reliance is a fundamental trait of Sigma males and is essential for their personal and professional growth.

In conclusion, solitude is essential for Sigma males as it allows them to recharge their mental and emotional batteries, be introspective, enhance creativity and productivity, pursue their interests and hobbies, and promote self-reliance and independence. Solitude is not a sign of weakness, isolation, or introversion. Instead, it is a tool that Sigma males use to enhance their personal growth, development, and success. Solitude enables Sigma males to be themselves, explore their thoughts and ideas, and pursue their passions without external distractions, pressures, or judgments. Therefore, Sigma males should embrace solitude as a valuable and necessary part of their lives.

5.2 Balancing Social Interaction with Alone Time

As a Sigma male, you are likely someone who values your alone time more than most. You may find that social interaction can be draining, and that you need ample time to recharge your batteries and reflect on your own thoughts and experiences. While there is nothing wrong with this, it is important to recognize that social interaction is an important aspect of life, and that finding a balance between socializing and spending time alone can be key to leading a fulfilling life.

One of the biggest challenges that Sigma males face when it comes to balancing social interaction with alone time is finding the right balance. On one hand, you may feel that you need more alone time than other people in order to feel centered and focused. On the other hand, you don't want to miss out on important interactions with friends, family members, and colleagues.

One way to find a balance is to make sure that you are scheduling enough time for both social interaction and alone time. This means making sure that you are carving out time in your schedule for social events, meetings, and other activities that require you to be around other people. At the same time, you should make sure that you are setting aside enough time to be alone, whether that means taking a solo walk, reading a book, or engaging in another activity that helps you recharge.

Another important aspect of balancing social interaction with alone time is being mindful of your own needs and boundaries. While it is important to be social and engage with others, it is also important to recognize when you are feeling overwhelmed or overstimulated. If you find that you are feeling exhausted or drained after a social event or interaction, it may be time to take a break and spend some time alone. This can help you recharge and refocus, and can also help prevent burnout and other negative consequences of overexertion.

Another key aspect of balancing social interaction with alone time is being intentional about the types of social interactions you engage in. As a Sigma male, you may find that you prefer smaller, more intimate gatherings to larger, more chaotic ones. You may also find that you are more comfortable in one-on-one conversations than in large group settings. By being intentional about the types of social interactions you engage in, you can ensure that you are getting the most out of your social interactions while still honoring your need for alone time.

It is also important to recognize that balancing social interaction with alone time is not a one-size-fits-all proposition. What works for one person may not work for another, and what works for you may change over time. This means that you need to be flexible and adaptable when it comes to finding a balance that works for you. You may need to experiment with different approaches and strategies until you find the right mix of social interaction and alone time that allows you to thrive.

At the end of the day, balancing social interaction with alone time is all about finding a balance that works for you. It is about recognizing your own needs and limitations, being intentional about the types of social interactions you engage in, and being flexible and adaptable as your needs change over time. By finding the right balance, you can ensure that you are getting the most out of life, while still honoring your need for solitude and reflection.

5.3 Creativity and Productivity in Solitude

Solitude is an essential aspect of the Sigma Male's life. Sigma Males thrive in isolation, and they need it to recharge and refuel their inner selves. In solitude, Sigma Males can explore their creativity, develop their skills, and pursue their passions without the distractions and pressures of the outside world.

Creativity is one of the most significant benefits of solitude. Sigma Males are creative individuals who can produce unique and innovative ideas, concepts, and solutions. They are not afraid to think outside the box and explore unconventional and untested paths. However, creativity is not something that happens overnight. It takes time, effort, and a lot of practice to develop.

Solitude offers Sigma Males the time and space they need to cultivate their creative skills. In solitude, Sigma Males can focus their minds on their thoughts, ideas, and imaginations without interruption or distraction. They can experiment with different approaches, techniques, and styles until they find what works best for them.

Moreover, solitude allows Sigma Males to develop their skills and expertise without the pressure of external expectations. Sigma Males are independent, and they prefer to work on their own terms and pace. In solitude, Sigma Males can set their own goals, timelines, and standards without worrying about pleasing others or meeting someone else's expectations.

Productivity is another essential aspect of solitude. Sigma Males are productive individuals who can accomplish a lot in a short amount of time. They are efficient, focused, and disciplined, and they know how to manage their time and energy effectively. However, productivity is not an innate quality. It requires discipline, planning, and perseverance.

Solitude offers Sigma Males the environment they need to be productive. In solitude, Sigma Males can eliminate distractions, prioritize their tasks, and focus on their goals without interruption or interference. They can create a work environment that suits their preferences and needs, whether it's a quiet and organized space or a dynamic and energetic one.

Moreover, solitude allows Sigma Males to work on their projects without interruptions or distractions. Sigma Males are independent individuals who prefer to work alone and undisturbed. They find it challenging to work in groups or teams, where their ideas and preferences may be ignored or dismissed. In solitude, Sigma Males can work on their projects at their own pace and rhythm without worrying about external interference or criticism.

However, solitude is not always easy to achieve. In today's world, where social media, instant messaging, and constant connectivity are the norm, solitude can be a rare and elusive commodity. Sigma Males may find it challenging to disconnect from the outside world and create a space for themselves where they can be alone and undisturbed.

Moreover, Sigma Males may face external pressures and expectations that make solitude difficult to achieve. Society values extroversion, sociability, and teamwork, and Sigma Males may feel pressured to conform to these norms even if they don't feel comfortable with them. Sigma Males may be judged or criticized for their independent and introverted nature, which may make them feel isolated and misunderstood.

However, Sigma Males should not be discouraged by these challenges. Solitude is an essential aspect of their identity and their well-being, and they should strive to achieve it despite the obstacles. Sigma Males should prioritize their need for solitude and create a space for themselves where they can be alone and undisturbed. They should also communicate their needs and preferences to their friends, family, and colleagues, so they can understand and respect their boundaries.

In conclusion, solitude is a vital aspect of the Sigma Male's life. It offers them the opportunity to explore their creativity, develop their skills, and pursue their passions without external interference or pressure. It also allows them to be productive, efficient, and focused on their goals. However, solitude can be challenging to achieve in today's world, where social norms and external pressures favor extroversion and sociability. Sigma Males should prioritize their need for solitude and create a space for themselves where they can be alone and undisturbed. They should also communicate their needs and preferences to others, so they can understand and respect their boundaries. Solitude is not a weakness or a flaw; it is a strength and a virtue that Sigma Males should embrace and celebrate.

5.4 Embracing Solitude Without Isolation

The need for solitude is one of the defining characteristics of the Sigma Male. Unlike their Alpha and Beta counterparts, Sigma Males crave alone time, and they need it to recharge their batteries, reflect on their lives and goals, and find inspiration and creativity. However, there is a fine line between solitude and isolation, and Sigma Males must learn to embrace solitude without becoming isolated from the world around them.

Solitude is a state of being alone, but it does not necessarily mean loneliness or disconnection from others. On the contrary, solitude can be a powerful tool for building strong relationships, deepening one's understanding of oneself and others, and cultivating empathy and compassion. For Sigma Males, solitude is a way to find peace and clarity in a world that can be chaotic, overwhelming, and demanding. It allows them to process their thoughts and emotions without external distractions or influences, to explore new ideas and perspectives, and to connect with their inner selves and higher purpose.

However, solitude can also become a trap if it turns into isolation. Isolation is a state of being cut off from others, emotionally, physically, or socially. It can lead to loneliness, depression, anxiety, and other mental health issues, and it can hinder personal and professional growth and fulfillment. For Sigma Males, isolation can be a double-edged sword. On one hand, it can provide a sense of safety and control in a world that can be hostile and unpredictable. On the other hand, it can lead to a sense of detachment from reality, a lack of social skills and emotional intelligence, and a narrow-minded perspective.

The key to embracing solitude without isolation is to find a balance between the two. Sigma Males must learn to enjoy their alone time without neglecting their social and emotional needs. They must cultivate healthy relationships with others, even if they prefer to spend most of their time alone. They must engage in meaningful activities and hobbies that inspire them and challenge them, even if they require interaction with others. They must be open to new experiences and perspectives, even if they contradict their own beliefs and values. And they must learn to communicate effectively and empathetically, even if it goes against their natural tendency to be reserved and independent.

One way to achieve this balance is to practice mindfulness. Mindfulness is a state of being aware of one's thoughts, feelings, and sensations in the present moment, without judgment or attachment. It can help Sigma Males stay grounded and focused, even in the midst of chaos and stress. It can also help them build resilience and compassion towards themselves and others, and develop a deeper sense of purpose and meaning in life.

Another way to achieve this balance is to seek out like-minded individuals and communities. Sigma Males may feel like they are the only ones who value solitude and independence, but in reality, there are many others who share their lifestyle and philosophy. By connecting with others who understand and respect their need for alone time, Sigma Males can build a support network that enhances their sense of belonging and purpose. They can also share their knowledge, skills, and experiences with others who can benefit from their insights and perspectives.

A third way to achieve this balance is to set boundaries and priorities. Sigma Males must learn to say "no" to social obligations and activities that do not align with their values or goals. They must also learn to prioritize their alone time and creative pursuits over external demands and distractions. This may require some sacrifice and discomfort at first, but in the long run, it will lead to a more fulfilling and authentic life.

In conclusion, embracing solitude without isolation is a crucial skill for Sigma Males to master. By finding a balance between alone time and social engagement, mindfulness and community, and boundaries and priorities, Sigma Males can live a life that is both independent and meaningful. They can cultivate their unique talents and passions, while also enriching the lives of others and contributing to the greater good. Solitude may be a solitary path, but it does not have to be a lonely one. With the right mindset and practices, Sigma Males can thrive in a world that values connection and collaboration, without compromising their true nature and identity.

5.5 Cultivating Deep and Meaningful Relationships as a Sigma Male

Being a Sigma Male does not mean that you cannot have deep and meaningful relationships. However, it does mean that you have a different approach to relationships than other males. As a Sigma Male, you value your alone time and independence, but this does not mean that you do not value human connection. In fact, meaningful relationships are important to you. You just require a different approach to cultivating and maintaining them.

One of the things that set Sigma Males apart from other males is that they tend to be highly selective in their relationships. They do not want to waste their time and energy on people who do not add value to their lives. This means that they are highly discerning in their choice of friends, romantic partners, and business associates.

When it comes to friendships, Sigma Males tend to have a small but tight circle of friends. They value quality over quantity and prefer to have a few friends who they can trust and rely on. These friends are usually people who share similar values and interests as the Sigma Male. They enjoy spending time together and have a deep understanding of each other.

In romantic relationships, Sigma Males tend to be highly selective as well. They do not want to waste their time on casual flings or short-term relationships. They prefer to take their time and find someone who they can truly connect with on a deep level. They value emotional intimacy and want to build a long-lasting and meaningful relationship with their partner.

One of the challenges that Sigma Males face in romantic relationships is that they can come across as aloof or distant. This is because they tend to keep their emotions close to the vest and do not like to reveal too much too soon. They value their independence and do not want to become too attached too quickly. However, once they do open up, they can be incredibly loyal and devoted partners.

Sigma Males also value their independence in business relationships. They do not want to be tied down to any one company or organization and prefer to work on their own terms. They tend to be highly entrepreneurial and enjoy taking risks and pursuing their passions. They are not afraid to go against the grain and do things differently than others.

When it comes to cultivating and maintaining relationships, Sigma Males have a few key strategies that they use. One of the most important is to be authentic and genuine in their interactions with others. They do not like to put on a false front or pretend to be someone they are not. They want to be accepted for who they are and value others who are the same way.

Another important strategy for Sigma Males is to be a good listener. They value deep and meaningful conversations and enjoy getting to know others on a deeper level. They are not interested in small talk or surface-level interactions. They want to understand what makes others tick and learn from their experiences.

Sigma Males also tend to be highly empathetic and compassionate. They understand that everyone has their own struggles and challenges and want to support others in their journey. They do not like to judge others or criticize them for their choices. Instead, they try to understand where others are coming from and offer support and guidance when needed.

In order to maintain their relationships, Sigma Males need to be able to balance their need for independence with their need for connection. They need to be able to communicate their needs and boundaries clearly to others and be willing to compromise when necessary. They also need to be able to make time for their relationships and prioritize them as an important part of their life.

Overall, Sigma Males have a unique approach to relationships that sets them apart from other males. They value quality over quantity and prefer deep and meaningful connections over surface-level interactions. They are highly discerning in their choice of friends, romantic partners, and business associates and tend to be highly independent and entrepreneurial. However, they also value their connections with others and are willing to put in the effort to cultivate and maintain those relationships.

5.6 Setting Boundaries and Communicating Your Need for Alone Time

In a world where socialization is constantly emphasized and extroversion is often praised, the sigma male stands out as a unique individual who values his alone time. While some people may see this need for solitude as anti-social behavior or a sign of weakness, the sigma male understands that it is an essential part of their well-being.

One of the most important aspects of embracing solitude is setting boundaries. It is essential to communicate your need for alone time to those around you, whether it is your friends, family or colleagues. This can be done in a respectful and considerate way, so that others can understand why you need to have some time to yourself.

Setting boundaries also involves being clear about what you are comfortable with and what you are not. For example, if you prefer not to have people drop by unannounced, it is important to make that clear to your friends and family. This can be done by simply saying something like "Hey, I really appreciate your company, but I need some alone time right now. Could we schedule some time to catch up later?"

Another way to set boundaries is to have a designated "alone time" space. This could be a room in your house, a specific spot in a park or any other location that makes you feel comfortable and at peace. By having a designated space for solitude, you can send a clear message to those around you that you need some time to yourself and that you value this time.

Another important aspect of setting boundaries is learning to say "no". This can be difficult for some people, especially those who value their relationships and want to please others. However, saying "no" when you need to is essential in setting healthy boundaries and ensuring you have the time and space you need to recharge.

In addition to setting boundaries, it is also important to communicate your need for alone time. This can be done in a variety of ways, depending on the situation. For example, if you are feeling overwhelmed at work, you could let your boss know that you need some time to work independently and recharge your batteries. Alternatively, if you are feeling drained after socializing with friends, you could explain that you need some alone time to decompress and recharge.

Communicating your need for alone time also involves being honest with yourself about your limits. It is important to recognize when you are feeling drained or burnt out and take the time you need to recharge. This may involve saying no to social invitations or taking a day off work to relax and rejuvenate.

At times, it may be difficult to communicate your need for alone time to those around you, especially if they are not used to the idea of solitude. However, it is important to remember that setting boundaries and communicating your needs is essential for your well-being. By doing so, you are not only taking care of yourself, but also setting a positive example for those around you.

In conclusion, setting boundaries and communicating your need for alone time is an essential part of embracing solitude as a sigma male. By being clear about your boundaries, communicating your needs and being honest with yourself about your limits, you can ensure that you have the time and space you need to recharge and thrive. While it may take some practice to get comfortable with setting boundaries and communicating your needs, it is a skill that will benefit you in all areas of your life.

5.7 Tips for Making the Most of Your Alone Time as a Sigma Male

The Sigma Male is often misunderstood by society, as they are individuals who prefer to be alone and are independent in nature. The need for solitude is important to Sigma Males, as it provides them with the opportunity to recharge their batteries and focus on their individual pursuits. However, it can be challenging for some Sigma Males to make the most of their alone time, as they may find themselves feeling restless or unproductive. In this paragraph, we will explore some tips for Sigma Males to maximize their alone time and achieve their goals.

1. Set specific goals

Sigma Males thrive on independence and self-direction. One way to make the most of alone time is to set specific goals for oneself. These goals can be personal or professional, but they should be challenging and achievable. When Sigma Males have a clear idea of what they want to accomplish during their alone time, they are more likely to stay focused and motivated. Goals can be short-term or long-term, but it is important to break them down into smaller, more manageable tasks to avoid feeling overwhelmed.

2. Cultivate hobbies and interests

Sigma Males are known for their individuality and independence. One way to make the most of alone time is to cultivate hobbies and interests that align with one's personal values and passions. Whether it is reading, writing, painting, or playing music, engaging in activities that bring joy and fulfillment can be a great way to recharge and refocus. By making time for these activities during alone time, Sigma Males can prioritize their own needs and interests.

3. Disconnect from technology

In today's hyper-connected world, it can be challenging to disconnect from technology, but doing so can be a powerful way to maximize alone time. Sigma Males may find it helpful to turn off their phones, computers, and other devices during their alone time to minimize distractions and focus more fully on their goals and interests. This may involve setting specific times for checking email or social media, or even taking a break from technology altogether. By disconnecting from technology, Sigma Males can create space for introspection, creativity, and self-discovery.

4. Practice mindfulness

Mindfulness is the practice of being fully present and engaged in the current moment. Sigma Males may find it helpful to incorporate mindfulness practices into their alone time, such as meditation, yoga, or breathing exercises. These practices can help reduce stress and anxiety, increase focus and concentration, and improve overall well-being. By practicing mindfulness during alone time, Sigma Males can cultivate a deeper sense of awareness and connection with themselves.

5. Embrace solitude

For Sigma Males, solitude is not something to be feared or avoided, but rather embraced and celebrated. Alone time provides a precious opportunity for self-reflection, introspection, and personal growth. By viewing solitude as a positive and valuable experience, Sigma Males can make the most of their alone time and develop a stronger sense of self-awareness and resilience.

6. Seek out new experiences

While Sigma Males may prefer to spend time alone, it is still important to seek out new experiences and opportunities for growth. This may involve trying new hobbies or activities, attending social events or networking opportunities, or even traveling to new places. By stepping outside of one's comfort zone and taking risks, Sigma Males can challenge themselves to grow and evolve in new and exciting ways.

7. Take care of physical health

Physical health is an essential aspect of overall well-being, and Sigma Males may find it helpful to prioritize their health during alone time. This may involve regular exercise, healthy eating habits, or engaging in activities that promote relaxation and stress reduction, such as yoga or meditation. By taking care of one's physical health during alone time, Sigma Males can improve their energy levels, mental clarity, and overall quality of life.

In conclusion, alone time is a crucial aspect of the Sigma Male's lifestyle, and by following these tips, Sigma Males can make the most of their alone time and achieve their goals. By setting specific goals, cultivating hobbies and interests, disconnecting from technology, practicing mindfulness, embracing solitude, seeking out new experiences, and taking care of physical health, Sigma Males can prioritize their own needs and interests and achieve personal growth and fulfillment.

6. The Sigma Male's Approach to Health and Wellness

6.1 Prioritizing Physical Health

The Sigma Male's Approach to Health and Wellness prioritizes physical health as an essential component of overall well-being. Physical health is a critical aspect of life that affects our mental, emotional, and social well-being. The Sigma Male understands that taking care of the body is crucial to living a fulfilling life, achieving goals, and being independent.

Physical health encompasses various dimensions, including exercise, nutrition, and rest. The Sigma Male recognizes the importance of maintaining a healthy body by adopting healthy habits that support physical well-being. Regular exercise is a crucial component of physical health, and the Sigma Male embraces it as a lifestyle, not just a routine. Exercise releases endorphins, which improve mood, boost energy, and promote better sleep. Additionally, it helps to strengthen muscles, improve cardiovascular health, and maintain a healthy weight.

The Sigma Male understands that exercise is not a one-size-fits-all approach. Each individual has unique needs, and it is essential to find the right type of exercise that suits one's preferences and body type. The Sigma Male takes the time to identify the best exercises that work for him and makes exercise a regular part of his routine. He also understands the importance of consistency and discipline in maintaining an exercise routine, even when faced with obstacles such as a busy work schedule or lack of motivation.

In addition to exercise, nutrition is another critical component of physical health. The Sigma Male understands that the body needs a balanced and nutritious diet to function optimally. He recognizes the importance of eating a variety of foods, including fruits, vegetables, whole grains, and lean proteins. He avoids processed foods, sugary drinks, and excessive alcohol consumption, which can negatively impact physical health.

The Sigma Male also understands that maintaining good nutrition habits is not always easy. He takes the time to plan meals, cook healthy food, and avoid eating out excessively. He also recognizes the importance of portion control and moderation in maintaining a healthy diet.

Rest and sleep are also essential components of physical health. The Sigma Male understands that rest and sleep are crucial for the body to recover and heal. He prioritizes getting adequate sleep each day and recognizes the importance of quality sleep. He also understands that rest is not just about sleep but also includes taking breaks, relaxing, and engaging in activities that promote physical and mental well-being.

The Sigma Male also recognizes that physical health is not just about the body but also includes taking care of one's mental health. Mental health is a critical component of overall well-being and affects how one thinks, feels, and behaves. The Sigma Male takes steps to maintain good mental health by engaging in activities that promote relaxation, such as meditation, yoga, or other mindfulness practices. He also seeks professional help if he experiences mental health challenges such as anxiety, depression, or stress.

In conclusion, prioritizing physical health is a critical aspect of The Sigma Male's Approach to Health and Wellness. The Sigma Male understands that physical health is not just about the body but also encompasses mental, emotional, and social well-being. He recognizes the importance of regular exercise, a balanced and nutritious diet, adequate rest and sleep, and taking care of mental health. By adopting healthy habits that support physical well-being, The Sigma Male can live a fulfilling life, achieve his goals, and be independent.

6.2 Mental Health Matters: The Importance of Self-Care

When it comes to the concept of self-care, the phrase might conjure up images of bubble baths, face masks, and spa days. However, self-care encompasses so much more than just the stereotypical images we see in advertisements. For Sigma males, self-care is a vital aspect of maintaining a healthy and balanced life. It is a way to prioritize mental and emotional well-being and to cultivate resilience in the face of life's challenges.

Self-care is especially important for Sigma males, who may be more prone to neglecting their mental and emotional needs due to their independent nature. As independent thinkers, Sigma males often prioritize their work and personal goals over their mental health. They might feel that taking time for themselves is a sign of weakness or that it takes away from their productivity. However, neglecting mental health can lead to burnout, depression, and anxiety, which can ultimately hinder one's ability to achieve their goals.

One of the most critical aspects of self-care for Sigma males is developing a sense of self-awareness. Self-awareness means having a deep understanding of one's emotions, thoughts, and behaviors. It's about recognizing when we are feeling stressed, anxious, or overwhelmed and taking the necessary steps to address those feelings. Sigma males may find it challenging to connect with their emotions or to express them, but it's crucial to take the time to understand them fully.

Self-care can take many forms, and it's essential to find what works best for each individual. Some common self-care practices may include meditation, journaling, and exercise. Meditation is a powerful tool that can help calm the mind and reduce stress. By taking just a few minutes each day to meditate, Sigma males can cultivate a sense of inner peace and clarity. Journaling can also be a useful practice for Sigma males, as it allows them to process their thoughts and emotions in a way that feels safe and private. Exercise is another important aspect of self-care, as it can boost mood and energy levels, leading to improved overall well-being.

Another critical element of self-care is setting boundaries. As Sigma males, it's easy to get caught up in work or personal projects and neglect relationships or other aspects of life that are important to us. However, setting boundaries is essential to avoid burnout and maintain healthy relationships. This might mean saying "no" to a project or social event, or taking a break from work to spend time with loved ones. By setting boundaries, Sigma males can ensure that they are not overextending themselves and can maintain a healthy work-life balance.

Finally, self-care involves being kind to ourselves. Sigma males often hold themselves to high standards and can be overly critical of their mistakes or shortcomings. However, self-compassion is crucial in maintaining a healthy mindset. Instead of beating ourselves up over mistakes, we can learn to treat ourselves with the same kindness and understanding that we offer to our friends and loved ones. By practicing self-compassion, Sigma males can improve their resilience and bounce back more easily from setbacks.

In conclusion, self-care is a critical aspect of maintaining mental and emotional well-being, particularly for Sigma males. By developing self-awareness, setting boundaries, and being kind to ourselves, we can prioritize our mental health and cultivate resilience in the face of life's challenges. Self-care is not just about bubble baths and face masks; it's a vital practice for achieving our goals and living a fulfilling life.

6.3 Exploring Alternative Health Practices

Sigma males often approach health and wellness in a non-traditional way, seeking out alternative health practices that may not be widely accepted or promoted by mainstream medicine. These practices often emphasize a holistic approach to health, incorporating physical, emotional, and spiritual well-being into their overall approach.

One major area of alternative health practices that sigma males often explore is nutrition. Many sigma males believe in the power of a plant-based diet to improve overall health and reduce the risk of chronic diseases such as heart disease, diabetes, and cancer. They may also experiment with different types of fasting, such as intermittent fasting or extended water fasts, in order to improve their health and longevity.

In addition to nutrition, many sigma males also explore alternative approaches to physical activity and fitness. Some may prefer more natural forms of exercise, such as hiking, swimming, or practicing martial arts, rather than going to a traditional gym. Others may incorporate yoga or meditation into their fitness routine, recognizing the benefits of these practices for both physical and mental health.

Sigma males may also explore alternative forms of healing, such as acupuncture, chiropractic, or energy healing. These practices are often focused on balancing the body's energy systems in order to promote healing and reduce pain and inflammation. While these practices may not be fully understood or accepted by mainstream medicine, many sigma males find them to be effective in treating a variety of health issues.

Another area of alternative health practices that sigma males may explore is mental health and wellness. Many sigma males recognize the importance of emotional well-being and seek out practices such as mindfulness meditation, therapy, or breathwork to help manage stress, anxiety, and depression. They may also explore alternative approaches to mental health, such as psychedelic therapy, in order to address deep-seated emotional issues and promote healing.

Overall, the sigma male's approach to health and wellness is characterized by a willingness to explore alternative practices and seek out holistic solutions to health issues. While these practices may not be fully accepted by mainstream medicine, sigma males are often driven by a desire to take control of their own health and well-being, and to find solutions that work for them personally. By taking a holistic approach to health, they are able to address both physical and emotional issues, promoting overall wellness and longevity.

6.4 Finding the Right Balance: Balancing Health and Independence

As a Sigma male, living a life of independence is essential to you. However, it's important to understand that independence doesn't mean neglecting your health. Finding the right balance between health and independence can be challenging, but it's essential for living a fulfilling life.

First, let's talk about the importance of health. Your health is your wealth. Without good health, you won't be able to enjoy your independence fully. Being healthy means having the energy and vitality to pursue your goals and enjoy life's simple pleasures. It also means being able to handle stress and challenges without breaking down physically or mentally.

As a Sigma male, you may be tempted to neglect your health to focus on your goals and ambitions. However, this approach is shortsighted and can lead to serious health problems down the line. It's essential to take care of your health now so that you can continue to enjoy your independence in the future.

So, what does it mean to balance health and independence? It means finding a way to pursue your goals and ambitions while also taking care of your physical, mental, and emotional health. Here are some tips for finding the right balance:

1. Prioritize your health

Make your health a priority. Don't put it off until tomorrow or next week. Schedule regular check-ups with your doctor and dentist. Eat a healthy diet, exercise regularly, and get enough sleep. If you have any health concerns, address them as soon as possible. It's better to catch a problem early than to wait until it becomes a more significant issue.

2. Take breaks

As a Sigma male, you may be tempted to work long hours without taking breaks. However, this approach can be detrimental to your health. Taking breaks throughout the day can help you recharge and improve your productivity. Take a walk, stretch, or do some deep breathing exercises. You'll come back to your work refreshed and ready to tackle the next task.

3. Practice self-care

Self-care is essential for maintaining good health. Make time for activities that bring you joy and relaxation. This could be anything from reading a book to taking a bubble bath. Whatever it is, make sure it's something that helps you unwind and recharge.

4. Manage stress

Stress is a part of life, but too much stress can be harmful to your health. Make an effort to manage your stress levels. This could be through exercise, meditation, or talking to a therapist. Find what works for you and make it a regular part of your routine.

5. Stay connected

As an independent male, you may be used to doing things on your own. However, it's essential to stay connected with others. Having a support system can help you manage stress, stay accountable for your health goals, and provide a sense of belonging. Make time for social activities and connect with friends and family regularly.

Finding the right balance between health and independence is an ongoing process. It's essential to be mindful of your health and make it a priority. By taking care of your physical, mental, and emotional well-being, you'll be better equipped to pursue your goals and live a fulfilling life.

6.5 Embracing a Minimalist Lifestyle for Health and Wellness

The Sigma Male's approach to health and wellness takes into account all aspects of their lives, including their living environment, work, and relationships. One important aspect that Sigma Males incorporate into their lifestyle is minimalism. Minimalism is not only about decluttering and simplifying their possessions but also about removing unnecessary stressors and distractions that can negatively impact their physical and mental health.

Minimalism is not just a trend; it is a way of life that can provide numerous benefits for a healthy and fulfilling life. Here are some ways in which embracing a minimalist lifestyle can improve health and wellness for Sigma Males:

Reduced Stress and Anxiety

Sigma Males often have many activities and responsibilities on their plate, and cluttered living spaces can add to their stress and anxiety levels. A minimalist lifestyle helps to eliminate unnecessary clutter, which provides a sense of calm and relaxation in their living spaces. The less clutter there is, the less the mind has to juggle and worry about. A calm and peaceful environment can help reduce stress and anxiety levels, leading to better mental health and overall well-being.

Improved Physical Health

Minimalism is not just about decluttering and simplifying possessions; it also extends to food, exercise, and self-care practices. Sigma Males who embrace minimalism often focus on the quality of the food they eat rather than the quantity. By consuming nutrient-dense foods, they can improve their physical health while reducing their carbon footprint. They may also embrace minimalist exercise routines such as yoga or bodyweight exercises to stay fit without requiring much equipment or gym memberships.

Improved Relationships

Minimalism encourages Sigma Males to focus on what's important in their lives, including relationships. By removing the distractions and clutter from their lives, they can focus on building and maintaining meaningful relationships with family and friends. Minimalism helps them to prioritize their time and focus on what truly matters, leading to deeper and more fulfilling relationships.

Financial Freedom

Minimalism is an excellent tool for achieving financial freedom. Sigma Males who embrace minimalism often avoid unnecessary purchases, leading to significant savings. This money can be used for experiences that bring joy and fulfillment rather than material possessions that may bring temporary pleasure. By practicing minimalism, Sigma Males can avoid falling into consumerism traps and have more control over their finances, leading to financial freedom and peace of mind.

Sustainable Living

Minimalism is not just about simplifying life; it is also about living sustainably. Sigma Males who embrace minimalism often opt for eco-friendly options, such as reusable bags, water bottles, and cloth napkins, reducing their carbon footprint. Minimalism encourages living with intention and avoiding wastefulness, leading to a more sustainable and mindful lifestyle.

Emotional and Mental Clarity

Minimalism helps Sigma Males to declutter not just their physical possessions but also their emotional and mental spaces. By removing distractions and unnecessary stressors from their lives, they can focus on what's truly important, leading to mental and emotional clarity. With this clarity, they can make better decisions, set meaningful goals, and pursue a fulfilling life.

Conclusion

Embracing a minimalist lifestyle can provide numerous benefits for Sigma Males' health and wellness. Minimalism is not just about decluttering and simplifying possessions; it is about living with intention, sustainability, and mindfulness. By removing unnecessary stressors and distractions, Sigma Males can improve their physical and mental health, build meaningful relationships, achieve financial freedom, and live a more fulfilling life.

6.6 Maintaining Healthy Habits: Tips for Staying on Track

The Sigma Male's approach to health and wellness is centered around independence, self-reliance, and discipline. These qualities are essential for maintaining healthy habits, which are key to living a fulfilling and productive life. However, staying on track with healthy habits can be challenging, especially in the face of temptation, stress, and distractions. In this section, we will explore some tips and strategies for staying on track with healthy habits.

Know your why

The first step in maintaining healthy habits is to understand why they are important to you. Ask yourself, "Why do I want to be healthy?" Is it to have more energy, to feel better physically and mentally, to live longer, or to set a good example for your family and community? Whatever your reasons may be, hold on to them and use them as motivation to stay on track. Write them down and keep them visible, so you can remind yourself of your why when you feel tempted to slip.

Set realistic goals

Setting goals is essential for staying on track with healthy habits. However, it's important to set realistic goals that are achievable and sustainable. Don't set yourself up for failure by aiming too high or too low. Instead, set short-term and long-term goals that are specific, measurable, and attainable. For instance, if you want to lose weight, set a goal of losing one to two pounds per week, rather than aiming to lose 20 pounds in a month. Celebrate your progress along the way and adjust your goals as needed.

Create a routine

Creating a routine is essential for maintaining healthy habits. When you have a routine, you are more likely to stick to it, even when life gets busy or stressful. Start by identifying the habits you want to establish, such as exercising, eating healthy, getting enough sleep, or meditating. Then, create a schedule that incorporates these habits into your daily or weekly routine. For instance, if you want to exercise four times a week, schedule your workouts at the same time each day or week, so you can establish a routine and make it a habit.

Hold yourself accountable

Holding yourself accountable is essential for staying on track with healthy habits. You are responsible for your own health and well-being, and nobody else can do it for you. One way to hold yourself accountable is to track your progress. Keep a journal, use an app, or create a spreadsheet to track your habits and progress. This will help you stay motivated and identify areas where you need to improve. Another way to hold yourself accountable is to enlist the support of others. Share your goals and progress with a friend, family member, or coach, who can provide encouragement, feedback, and accountability.

Practice self-care

Self-care is essential for maintaining healthy habits. When you take care of yourself, you are better equipped to handle stress, temptation, and distractions. Self-care can include anything that promotes physical, mental, or emotional well-being, such as taking a walk, reading a book, practicing yoga, or spending time with loved ones. Make self-care a priority in your routine, and don't be afraid to take a break or say no when you need to.

Avoid triggers

Avoiding triggers is essential for maintaining healthy habits. Triggers are anything that can lead to unhealthy behaviors, such as stress, boredom, negative emotions, or social pressure. Identify your triggers and find ways to avoid or manage them. For instance, if stress triggers you to eat unhealthy foods, find healthy ways to cope with stress, such as meditating, exercising, or talking to a friend. If social pressure leads you to drink too much alcohol, find alternative activities that don't involve alcohol, such as going to a movie or playing a game.

Stay motivated

Staying motivated is essential for maintaining healthy habits. Motivation can be challenging to maintain, especially when progress is slow or setbacks occur. However, there are ways to stay motivated and keep your eye on the prize. One way is to create a vision board, which is a visual representation of your goals and aspirations. Use images, words, and symbols to create a collage that represents your why and your goals. Hang it in a visible place, such as your bedroom or office, and look at it every day to stay motivated. Another way to stay motivated is to reward yourself for achieving milestones. Treat yourself to a massage, a movie, or a special meal when you reach a goal or make progress.

Conclusion

Maintaining healthy habits is essential for living a fulfilling and productive life. The Sigma Male's approach to health and wellness is centered around independence, self-reliance, and discipline. By knowing your why, setting realistic goals, creating a routine, holding yourself accountable, practicing self-care, avoiding triggers, and staying motivated, you can stay on track with healthy habits and achieve your goals. Remember, healthy habits are not a destination but a journey, so be patient, persistent, and resilient.

6.7 Navigating the Health Industry as a Sigma Male

The health industry is a complex and often overwhelming landscape to navigate. For a Sigma male, it can be particularly challenging since they often prefer to take an independent and self-sufficient approach to their health and wellness. However, with some knowledge and a strategic approach, Sigma males can successfully navigate the health industry.

The first step for Sigma males is to understand their own health needs and goals. This requires taking a holistic approach to health and wellness, looking beyond just physical health to include mental, emotional, and spiritual well-being. Sigma males should take the time to assess their health status and identify any areas that need improvement. This may involve consulting with a healthcare provider to get a baseline assessment of their health.

Once Sigma males have a clear understanding of their health needs and goals, they can begin to research and explore different options for meeting those needs. This can include traditional medicine, alternative therapies, and lifestyle changes. Sigma males should approach this research with an open mind, considering a variety of options and weighing the pros and cons of each.

When considering traditional medical options, Sigma males should take care to find healthcare providers who align with their values and approach to health. This may involve seeking out providers who take a holistic approach to health, or who are open to alternative therapies. Sigma males should also take an active role in their healthcare, asking questions and advocating for their own health needs.

For Sigma males who prefer alternative therapies, there are a plethora of options available, from acupuncture and chiropractic care to herbal remedies and meditation. However, it is important for Sigma males to do their research and find reputable practitioners who have the necessary training and qualifications. They should also be aware that alternative therapies may not be covered by insurance and can be costly.

In addition to traditional and alternative medical options, Sigma males should also focus on lifestyle changes that can improve their overall health and wellness. This can include adopting a healthy diet, getting regular exercise, reducing stress, and practicing self-care. Sigma males should set realistic goals for themselves and develop a plan for achieving those goals.

One of the challenges Sigma males may face in navigating the health industry is the pressure to conform to traditional gender roles and expectations. Men are often socialized to be stoic and self-sufficient, which can make it difficult for Sigma males to seek help when they need it. However, it is important for Sigma males to recognize that seeking help is a sign of strength, not weakness. They should be willing to ask for help and support when they need it.

Another challenge Sigma males may encounter is the stigma surrounding mental health. Men are often discouraged from expressing emotions or seeking help for mental health issues. However, it is important for Sigma males to prioritize their mental health and seek help if needed. This may involve talking to a therapist, joining a support group, or practicing mindfulness and self-care.

Finally, Sigma males should be aware of the potential pitfalls of the health industry, such as over-diagnosis, over-treatment, and the influence of pharmaceutical companies. They should approach healthcare decisions with a critical eye and be willing to ask questions and seek second opinions. They should also be aware of the financial implications of healthcare decisions and consider the cost of treatments and procedures.

In conclusion, navigating the health industry as a Sigma male requires a holistic approach to health and wellness, a willingness to do research and explore different options, and an openness to seeking help when needed. By prioritizing their health needs and goals, and taking an active role in their healthcare, Sigma males can successfully navigate the health industry and maintain their independence and self-sufficiency.

6.8 The Role of Diet in Health and Wellness for Sigma Males

The Sigma Male's Approach to Health and Wellness is a crucial aspect of his overall persona. The Sigma Male is known for his independent nature, and this trait extends to his approach to health and wellness. He believes in taking charge of his health and wellbeing, and this includes paying careful attention to his diet.

The Role of Diet in Health and Wellness for Sigma Males is critical since food is the fuel that the body needs to function correctly. A Sigma Male understands this and makes sure that he is consuming the right foods to ensure optimal health. Eating the right foods is essential since it can help prevent chronic diseases such as heart disease, diabetes, and cancer.

A Sigma Male's diet should consist of whole foods that are rich in nutrients, including fruits, vegetables, whole grains, lean protein sources, and healthy fats. These foods contain vitamins, minerals, and antioxidants that are essential for good health. A Sigma Male understands that a well-rounded diet is necessary to maintain optimal health, energy levels, and mental clarity.

One of the key elements of a Sigma Male's diet is protein. Protein is essential for building and repairing muscles, and it is also important for maintaining healthy bones and tissues. A Sigma Male understands that the quality of protein matters, and he will opt for lean sources of protein such as chicken, fish, and plant-based sources like beans, lentils, and nuts.

A Sigma Male also understands that carbohydrates are not the enemy. Carbohydrates are essential for providing energy to the body, and they are necessary for performing physical activity. However, a Sigma Male will opt for complex carbohydrates such as whole grains, fruits, and vegetables, rather than simple carbohydrates like sugary foods and drinks.

Fats are another essential element of a Sigma Male's diet. Healthy fats, such as monounsaturated and polyunsaturated fats, are important for maintaining healthy cholesterol levels and reducing inflammation in the body. A Sigma Male will consume healthy fats from sources such as nuts, seeds, and avocados.

A Sigma Male also understands the importance of hydration. Drinking enough water is essential for maintaining good health, and it can also help with weight loss and digestion. A Sigma Male will make sure to drink enough water throughout the day, and he will opt for water over sugary drinks like soda and juice.

Another crucial aspect of a Sigma Male's diet is moderation. A Sigma Male understands that indulging in unhealthy foods occasionally is okay, but he will make sure not to overdo it. He will also avoid processed foods as much as possible, as they often contain unhealthy ingredients like added sugars and preservatives.

A Sigma Male will also pay attention to his portion sizes. Overeating can lead to weight gain and other health problems, so a Sigma Male will make sure to eat slowly, savor his food, and stop eating when he feels full.

In conclusion, Diet plays a critical role in the health and wellness of a Sigma Male. The right diet can help prevent chronic diseases, maintain energy levels and mental clarity, and support optimal health. A Sigma Male understands that a well-rounded diet that includes whole foods, lean protein sources, complex carbohydrates, healthy fats, and adequate hydration is necessary to achieve optimal health. He also understands the importance of moderation and portion control. By following a healthy diet, a Sigma Male can take charge of his health and wellbeing and continue to thrive in all aspects of life.

6.9 The Importance of Sleep for the Sigma Male

The Sigma Male is a unique personality type that values independence, self-reliance, and individuality. They often feel the need to carve their own path in life and do things their way. While this independent streak can lead to success in many areas, it can also come with downsides. One of the most important aspects of a healthy and well-rounded life is getting enough sleep. In this chapter, we will explore the importance of sleep for the Sigma Male and how they can optimize their sleep habits to live their best life.

Sleep is one of the most important factors in maintaining good health and wellbeing. Getting enough sleep can help improve memory, boost mood, increase productivity, and reduce the risk of chronic diseases such as diabetes and heart disease. While the exact amount of sleep needed varies from person to person, most adults need between 7-9 hours of sleep per night to function at their best.

For Sigma Males, getting enough sleep can be particularly important. Their independent nature often leads to a busy and high-pressure lifestyle that can be mentally and physically exhausting. However, given their tendency to prioritize work or personal projects over rest, Sigma Males may not get the amount of sleep they need to function at their best. This can lead to decreased productivity, decreased focus, and a higher risk of burnout.

One of the reasons why sleep is so important for Sigma Males is that it helps them recharge their mental batteries. Sigma Males are often deep thinkers who value their time alone, and sleep is an essential component of this mental restoration process. During sleep, the brain processes and consolidates memories, helps repair cell damage, and clears out toxins that have accumulated during the day. This means that getting enough sleep can lead to better mental clarity, improved cognitive function, and improved emotional resilience.

To optimize their sleep habits, Sigma Males should prioritize creating a sleep-friendly environment. This means minimizing distractions such as electronics, using comfortable bedding and pillows, and keeping the room at a cool and comfortable temperature. Additionally, Sigma Males should aim to create a consistent sleep routine that involves going to bed and waking up at the same time each day. This consistency can help regulate the body's internal clock and make it easier to fall asleep and wake up each day.

In addition to creating a sleep-friendly environment, Sigma Males should also consider incorporating relaxation techniques into their bedtime routine. This could include meditation, deep breathing exercises, or even a warm bath or shower. These relaxation techniques can help calm the mind and body, making it easier to fall asleep and stay asleep throughout the night.

In some cases, Sigma Males may struggle with sleep due to underlying medical issues such as sleep apnea or anxiety. If this is the case, seeking professional medical advice may be necessary to address these issues and improve sleep quality.

Overall, getting enough sleep is a crucial aspect of maintaining good health and wellbeing for Sigma Males. While their independent nature may lead them to prioritize work or personal projects over rest, getting enough sleep can actually improve productivity and mental clarity in the long run. By prioritizing a sleep-friendly environment, creating a consistent sleep routine, and incorporating relaxation techniques into their bedtime routine, Sigma Males can optimize their sleep habits and improve their overall quality of life.

6.10 Incorporating Fitness into Independent Living

As a Sigma male, you value your independence and self-sufficiency in all aspects of your life. However, this can sometimes lead to neglecting your health and fitness, as you focus on other areas of your life, such as work, hobbies, or relationships. Incorporating fitness into your independent living can help you maintain your physical and mental well-being, enhance your productivity and creativity, and improve your overall quality of life.

The first step in incorporating fitness into your independent living is to set realistic and achievable goals. Whether you want to lose weight, build muscle, improve your endurance, or simply be more active, you need to define your objectives and design a plan that suits your lifestyle, preferences, and abilities. You can consult with a fitness professional, use online resources, or join a fitness community to get inspiration, guidance, and feedback.

The second step in incorporating fitness into your independent living is to make it a habit. You need to commit to a regular schedule of exercise, whether it's daily, weekly, or monthly, and stick to it regardless of your mood, weather, or other distractions. You can choose the type of exercise that you enjoy the most, such as walking, running, cycling, swimming, weightlifting, yoga, or dancing, and vary your routine to avoid boredom and plateaus.

The third step in incorporating fitness into your independent living is to integrate it into your daily routine. You can incorporate physical activity into your work, leisure, and household tasks, such as taking the stairs instead of the elevator, walking or biking to work or errands, doing stretches or calisthenics during breaks, gardening, cleaning, or playing with your pets or kids. By making fitness a natural part of your lifestyle, you can save time, money, and effort, and maximize your health benefits.

The fourth step in incorporating fitness into your independent living is to monitor your progress and adjust your goals and plans accordingly. You can track your weight, body composition, strength, endurance, flexibility, and other fitness parameters, and use apps, journals, or charts to visualize your improvements and challenges. You can also seek feedback from your peers, family, or professionals, and use their input to refine your approach and motivation.

The fifth and final step in incorporating fitness into your independent living is to celebrate your achievements and maintain your momentum. You can reward yourself for reaching your milestones, whether it's buying new workout clothes, treating yourself to a massage or a healthy meal, or sharing your success with others. You can also challenge yourself to new goals and experiences, such as running a marathon, hiking a mountain, or learning a new sport or dance. By staying motivated and inspired, you can make fitness a lifelong passion and priority.

Incorporating fitness into your independent living can have numerous benefits for your physical and mental health, as well as your personal and professional development. By being proactive and intentional about your fitness, you can enhance your energy, focus, and creativity, reduce your stress, anxiety, and depression, boost your immune system, and prevent or manage chronic diseases. You can also improve your social skills, confidence, and attractiveness, as well as your career prospects, by being fit and healthy.

As a Sigma male, you may face some challenges in incorporating fitness into your independent living, such as lack of time, motivation, or resources, or social pressure to conform to certain standards or expectations. However, you can overcome these obstacles by adopting a growth mindset, seeking support and guidance from like-minded individuals, and focusing on your own goals and values. You can also inspire and motivate others by leading by example, sharing your knowledge and experience, and encouraging them to embrace their own fitness journey.

In conclusion, incorporating fitness into your independent living is an essential aspect of your health and wellness as a Sigma male. By setting realistic and achievable goals, making it a habit, integrating it into your daily routine, monitoring your progress, and celebrating your achievements, you can enhance your physical and mental well-being, and maintain your independence and self-sufficiency. You can also inspire and empower others to embrace their own fitness journey, and make a positive impact on the world around you.

7. Overcoming the Stigma: Misconceptions About Sigma Males

7.1 The Myth of the Anti-Social Sigma Male

The term "sigma male" is relatively new to the lexicon of personality types, and naturally, there are many misunderstandings and misconceptions about what it means to be a sigma male. One of the most persistent myths about the sigma male is that he is anti-social or a loner. This couldn't be further from the truth.

In fact, the sigma male is often more social than his alpha and beta counterparts, but in a different way. He is not interested in establishing dominance over others, nor is he interested in conforming to societal norms. Instead, he seeks out deep, meaningful connections with others on his own terms.

The stereotype of the anti-social sigma male likely stems from the fact that he is often independent and self-sufficient. He doesn't need others to validate his worth, and he is perfectly content spending time alone or with a small group of close friends. However, this doesn't mean he doesn't enjoy spending time with others or doesn't have strong social skills. The sigma male simply chooses his social interactions more carefully than others.

The sigma male's independence is often a result of his confidence in his own abilities and decision-making skills. He trusts himself and doesn't need constant input or validation from others. This can come across as anti-social or aloof to those who don't understand the sigma mentality.

However, the sigma male is not averse to socializing or forming connections with others. He simply approaches it differently. He values authenticity and honesty, and he is unlikely to form superficial or insincere relationships. Instead, he seeks out individuals who share his values and interests, and with whom he can form deeper connections.

Another reason the sigma male is often misconstrued as anti-social is that he doesn't conform to traditional social norms or hierarchies. He doesn't seek out approval from others, nor does he feel the need to fit in with a particular group. This can make it seem like he is disinterested or standoffish to those who don't understand his perspective.

However, the sigma male's non-conformity is actually a strength. He is able to think for himself and make decisions that align with his values and goals, rather than simply following the crowd. This independence and self-reliance are what set the sigma male apart from his peers and make him a valuable asset in any situation.

The sigma male's focus on authenticity and independence also means that he is unlikely to engage in social games or drama. He is not interested in petty disputes or jockeying for position within a group. This can again be misconstrued as anti-social or disinterested, but in reality, it is simply a reflection of the sigma male's focus on what truly matters to him.

In conclusion, the myth of the anti-social sigma male is just that – a myth. While the sigma male may be independent and self-sufficient, he is not averse to socializing or forming connections with others. He simply approaches it in his own way, with a focus on authenticity and deep connections rather than superficial social games. The sigma male's non-conformity and independence are strengths, not weaknesses, and should be celebrated rather than misunderstood.

7.2 The Misunderstood Lone Wolf

Sigma males are often characterized as lone wolves. They are seen as independent, self-sufficient individuals who prefer to operate on their own. However, this perception is often misunderstood and has led to misconceptions about sigma males. The truth is, sigma males do not necessarily prefer to be alone but are more comfortable operating independently when necessary. They have a strong sense of self and are self-reliant, but they are not necessarily anti-social or introverted.

Sigma males are often misunderstood because they do not conform to the traditional alpha or beta male archetype. They are not interested in asserting dominance over others or seeking approval from the group. Instead, they focus on achieving their goals and pursuing their passions. This can lead to them being seen as aloof or distant, but in reality, they are simply focused on their own growth and development.

Another misconception about sigma males is that they are not team players. While it is true that they prefer to work independently, they are still able to collaborate effectively with others. Sigma males are not interested in leading a group but are more than happy to contribute their skills and expertise to a team project. They are able to work well with others, but they also know when to step back and allow others to take charge.

Sigma males are also often perceived as being unemotional or cold. This is not necessarily true, as sigma males are simply more reserved when it comes to expressing their emotions. They do not feel the need to wear their heart on their sleeve and prefer to keep their emotional life private. This does not mean that they are incapable of feeling emotions, but rather they choose to express them in different ways. They may be more likely to show their emotions through actions rather than words.

Another misconception about sigma males is that they are not interested in forming relationships. While it is true that they value their independence, they are still capable of forming deep and meaningful connections with others. However, they do not seek out relationships for the sake of having them. Instead, they are more interested in forming connections with people who align with their values and goals. They are not interested in superficial relationships and prefer to invest their time and energy in those who they feel a genuine connection with.

In addition, sigma males are often seen as being arrogant or self-centered. This is not necessarily true, as sigma males are simply confident in their abilities and value their own opinions. They do not feel the need to seek validation from others and are comfortable standing behind their decisions. However, they are not dismissive of others' opinions and are open to hearing different perspectives. They simply trust their own judgment and are not easily swayed by the opinions of others.

It is important to understand that sigma males are not always easy to categorize. They do not fit neatly into a specific mold and are often misunderstood as a result. However, by taking the time to understand their unique qualities and characteristics, it becomes clear that they are not lone wolves in the traditional sense. They are simply individuals who value their independence and are not afraid to pursue their own path in life. They are capable of forming deep and meaningful connections with others and are not dismissive of the opinions of those around them. Sigma males are complex individuals who defy easy categorization, but they are also some of the most interesting and dynamic people you will ever meet.

7.3 Dispelling the Idea of the Unemotional Sigma Male

The concept of a Sigma male is often surrounded by various misconceptions, particularly when it comes to the idea that they are unemotional, cold, and distant. These notions are not only incorrect but also paint a skewed picture of what it means to be a Sigma male. In this chapter, we will delve deeper into this misconception and dispel the idea of the unemotional Sigma male.

Firstly, it is essential to understand that being unemotional is not a characteristic of a Sigma male. Rather, it is a stereotype that has been perpetuated by society's popular media. The media often portrays Sigma males as emotionless beings who are incapable of connecting with others on an emotional level. This portrayal is far from the truth.

In reality, Sigma males are capable of experiencing a wide range of emotions, just like any other human being. However, they tend to process their emotions differently from others. Sigma males tend to be introspective and reflective, and therefore, they take their time to process their emotions. They are not quick to react or overreact to situations, but rather, they think through their emotions and consider the best course of action.

This introspective nature can often be mistaken for a lack of emotions, but in fact, it is quite the opposite. Sigma males feel deeply but choose to express their emotions in a more controlled and measured way. They prefer not to let their emotions control their actions and instead focus on finding solutions to problems.

Furthermore, Sigma males are often misconstrued as being cold and distant. This could not be further from the truth. Sigma males are independent, but this does not mean that they are not sociable or incapable of forming close relationships. In fact, Sigma males can be quite warm and welcoming. However, they tend to keep a small circle of friends and prefer to be selective in their social interactions.

Sigma males value their personal space and time, and therefore, they are not always open to socializing. However, when they do choose to socialize, they tend to be engaging and enjoyable. Sigma males may not always be the life of the party, but they can hold interesting conversations and provide valuable insights.

It is also crucial to note that Sigma males are not unempathetic or lacking in compassion. They may not show their emotions in the same way as others, but this does not mean that they do not care. Sigma males tend to be very observant and can sense the emotions of those around them. They may not always express their concerns verbally, but they often find ways to offer support and help to those who need it.

Another myth about Sigma males is that they are not romantic or interested in relationships. This is not true. Sigma males can be very romantic and are often interested in forming close relationships. However, they tend to be selective in their partner choices and prefer to take their time in getting to know someone before committing to a relationship.

Sigma males are independent and value their personal freedom, and therefore, they are not always looking for a committed relationship. However, when they do choose to commit, they tend to be loyal and devoted partners.

In conclusion, the idea of the unemotional Sigma male is a misconception that needs to be dispelled. Sigma males are not emotionless beings but rather individuals who process their emotions differently from others. They are not cold or distant but rather selective in their social interactions. Sigma males are not lacking in empathy or compassion and are capable of forming close relationships. They can be romantic and are often interested in committed relationships. It is time to break free from the stereotypes and myths surrounding Sigma males and recognize them for the independent, thoughtful, and emotionally intelligent individuals that they are.

7.4 The Real Reason Behind a Sigma Male's Independence

The Sigma male is often misunderstood by society. People often perceive them as lone wolves, introverted, and anti-social individuals who are arrogant and self-absorbed. However, these misconceptions are far from the truth. The Sigma male is a unique breed of human beings who are often intelligent, self-sufficient, and independent individuals who value their freedom and personal space. One of the key defining traits of a Sigma male is their independence. In this section, we will explore the real reason behind a Sigma Male's independence.

The Sigma male's independence can be attributed to various factors, such as their personality, upbringing, life experiences, and values. For instance, if a Sigma male grew up in a household where they were not given much attention, they tend to develop a strong sense of self-reliance. Hence, they tend to rely on themselves and avoid depending on others. Such individuals tend to develop a self-sufficient mindset, which inevitably leads to independence.

Furthermore, Sigma males tend to be highly introspective and self-aware individuals who understand their strengths and weaknesses. They value their personal space and privacy, and they tend to avoid relying too much on others. Consequently, they develop a sense of independence that allows them to be self-sufficient and autonomous.

Another factor that contributes to a Sigma male's independence is their ability to think critically and make informed decisions. Sigma males tend to be highly intelligent and analytical individuals who can evaluate a situation objectively. They tend to weigh the pros and cons of a decision before making a choice. This skill enables them to make informed decisions that align with their values and beliefs.

Sigma males also tend to be highly ambitious individuals who are not afraid to take risks. They have a clear vision of what they want to achieve in life, and they work hard to realize their goals. This ambition and drive enable them to pursue their dreams independently without relying on others.

Moreover, Sigma males tend to be highly adaptable individuals who can thrive in any environment. They are comfortable being alone, and they can function well in social situations. They tend to have a high degree of emotional intelligence, which enables them to read social cues and interact effectively with others. Hence, they can navigate social situations easily and independently.

Another reason why Sigma males value their independence is that they tend to have a low tolerance for drama and conflict. They avoid getting caught up in the drama of others, and they tend to keep their business to themselves. They do not seek validation from others and are comfortable with their choices and decisions. This trait enables them to avoid unnecessary conflict and drama and maintain their emotional well-being.

Furthermore, Sigma males tend to be highly self-disciplined individuals who can set goals and stick to them. They have a strong sense of purpose, which enables them to pursue their goals diligently. This self-discipline enables them to maintain their independence and avoid getting sidetracked by distractions.

In conclusion, the real reason behind a Sigma Male's independence is a combination of various factors, such as their personality, upbringing, life experiences, and values. Sigma males tend to be highly introspective and self-aware individuals who value their personal space and privacy. They tend to be highly ambitious individuals who are not afraid to take risks and pursue their dreams independently. Furthermore, they have a low tolerance for drama and conflict and tend to avoid getting caught up in the drama of others. They are highly adaptable individuals who can thrive in any environment and can navigate social situations easily and independently. Ultimately, the Sigma male's independence is a defining trait that enables them to be self-sufficient, autonomous, and successful individuals.

7.5 Breaking Down the Stereotype of the Sigma Male as a Commitment-Phobe

The Sigma Male is an archetype that has gained popularity over the years, yet there is still a lot of confusion surrounding it. One of the most prevalent misconceptions about Sigma Males is that they are commitment-phobes. This stereotype may have been fueled by the portrayal of Sigma Males in popular media as lone wolves who prefer to be alone rather than being in a relationship. However, the truth is that the Sigma Male is not a commitment-phobe, but rather, he is selective when it comes to relationships.

The Sigma Male's independence and self-sufficiency can often be interpreted as a reluctance to commit to a partner. However, this is far from the truth. Sigma Males are not adverse to relationships, but they value their freedom and independence above all else. They are not willing to compromise their individuality to fit into the traditional mold of a traditional relationship.

Sigma Males are often misunderstood because they do not conform to societal norms. They are not interested in pursuing the traditional path of settling down, getting married, and having kids. Instead, they prefer to live life on their own terms, following their passions and pursuing their goals without any restrictions.

The Sigma Male's commitment to their own independence can often be interpreted as a lack of commitment to a partner. However, this is not the case. The Sigma Male is committed to their partner as long as their partner shares their values and ambitions. They are not willing to compromise their individuality for the sake of a relationship.

The Sigma Male's selectiveness when it comes to relationships is often misconstrued as commitment-phobia. However, it is actually a sign of their strength and self-awareness. Sigma Males are not interested in settling for someone who does not share their values or passions. They are willing to wait for the right person to come along rather than wasting their time with someone who does not align with their goals and dreams.

The Sigma Male's self-sufficient nature can also be seen as a sign of their commitment to their partner. They do not rely on their partner to fulfill their emotional or financial needs. Instead, they are self-sufficient and self-reliant, making them a reliable partner who can support their partner through thick and thin.

Another misconception about Sigma Males is that they are emotionally detached. This could not be further from the truth. Sigma Males are deeply emotional and passionate individuals who value deep connections and meaningful relationships. However, they are selective about who they let into their inner circle. They do not waste their time or energy on shallow connections and meaningless relationships.

The Sigma Male's emotional intelligence and self-awareness are what make them such great partners. They are able to communicate their needs and emotions effectively, which leads to a deeper connection with their partner. They are not afraid to be vulnerable and share their emotions, which is a sign of strength and courage.

In conclusion, the stereotype of the Sigma Male as a commitment-phobe is a gross oversimplification of the complex nature of this archetype. Sigma Males are not afraid of commitment, but rather, they are selective when it comes to relationships. They value their independence and self-sufficiency above all else, but they are willing to commit to a partner who shares their values and ambitions. The Sigma Male's emotional intelligence and self-awareness are what make them such great partners, and their commitment to their own individuality is a sign of strength and courage. It is time to break down the stereotype of the Sigma Male as a commitment-phobe and embrace the complexity of this archetype.

7.6 The Truth About Sigma Males and Leadership

There are many misconceptions about Sigma males and leadership. Some people believe that Sigma males are not fit to lead because they are too independent and self-reliant. Others think that Sigma males lack the charisma and social skills needed to inspire and motivate others to follow them. However, these stereotypes are far from the truth.

The Sigma Male

In reality, Sigma males can be great leaders. They possess many qualities that are essential for effective leadership, such as intelligence, decisiveness, and resilience. They are also excellent problem-solvers and strategic thinkers, which makes them well-suited for positions of authority.

One of the main reasons why Sigma males make good leaders is their ability to remain calm and composed in stressful situations. Unlike Alpha males, who can become emotional and reactive when faced with adversity, Sigma males are able to stay level-headed and rational. This allows them to make sound decisions even in the face of uncertainty and chaos.

Another advantage that Sigma males have as leaders is their ability to think outside the box. Because they are not bound by the constraints of social norms and expectations, Sigma males are often able to come up with unconventional solutions to complex problems. This can be a huge asset in a leadership role, where creativity and innovation are valued.

Furthermore, Sigma males are known for their introspective nature. They are constantly analyzing their own thoughts and behaviors, which allows them to identify their strengths and weaknesses. This self-awareness is a valuable trait for a leader, as it enables them to identify areas where they need to improve and take steps to address those issues.

Despite these strengths, Sigma males can face some unique challenges when it comes to leadership. One of the biggest obstacles they face is their tendency to be introverted and socially reserved. While this trait can be an asset in some situations, it can also create difficulties when it comes to building relationships with team members and stakeholders.

To overcome this challenge, Sigma males need to be intentional about developing their interpersonal skills. They need to learn how to connect with others on a deeper level, and how to communicate their ideas and vision in a way that resonates with their audience. This may require pushing themselves out of their comfort zone and practicing social skills they may not be naturally inclined towards.

Another challenge that Sigma males face is their inclination towards individualism. While independence is an admirable trait, it can sometimes make it difficult for Sigma males to work effectively in a team environment. They may struggle to delegate tasks to others, or to trust their colleagues to handle important responsibilities.

To overcome this challenge, Sigma males need to learn how to balance their individualistic tendencies with the need to collaborate with others. They need to recognize the strengths and expertise of their team members, and learn how to leverage those strengths to achieve their shared goals. This may mean developing a greater sense of empathy and emotional intelligence, and learning how to build trust and rapport with others.

Overall, Sigma males have the potential to be great leaders. Their unique combination of intelligence, resilience, and creativity can be a huge asset in a leadership role. However, they may need to work on developing their interpersonal skills and their ability to work effectively in a team environment. With the right mindset and a commitment to self-improvement, Sigma males can overcome these challenges and thrive as leaders.

7.7 Challenging the Assumption that Sigma Males are Always Introverted

Sigma males have often been stereotyped as being introverted, reclusive, and lacking social skills. However, this assumption is far from accurate. While many sigma males may exhibit introverted tendencies, it is not a defining characteristic of the personality type. In reality, sigma males are just as likely to be extroverted and outgoing as they are to be introverted and reserved.

To begin with, it is important to understand what sigma males are, and what sets them apart from other male personality types. Sigma males are independent, self-reliant, and often exhibit traits associated with both alpha and beta males. They are confident, assertive, and ambitious, but also value their privacy and independence. Unlike alpha males, who thrive on social dominance and assert their authority over others, sigma males prefer to operate independently and avoid the attention that alpha males crave.

One of the biggest misconceptions about sigma males is that they are socially awkward or lack social skills. This could not be further from the truth. Sigma males often have a strong sense of self-awareness and are comfortable in their own skin. They are confident in their abilities and don't feel the need to prove themselves to others. While they may not always be the life of the party, they are typically well-liked and respected by those around them.

Another factor that challenges the assumption that sigma males are always introverted is that many sigma males are successful in social situations. They may not actively seek out attention or social interactions, but they are often comfortable in social settings and can be quite charming and engaging. While they may not be the most talkative person in the room, they are often excellent listeners and have a knack for making others feel heard and understood.

Furthermore, sigma males are not immune to the benefits of socializing and networking. While they may not prioritize social activities in the same way that alpha males do, they still recognize the importance of building relationships and connecting with others. In fact, many sigma males excel in networking and building professional relationships, as they are often able to avoid the power struggles and dominance games that alpha males engage in.

It is also important to note that introversion is not a negative trait. While many people assume that introverts are shy or socially awkward, introversion simply refers to a preference for solitude and reflection. Introverted sigma males may enjoy spending time alone, but that does not mean they lack social skills or the ability to interact with others. In fact, introverted sigma males may be more comfortable in social situations that are focused on intellectual or creative pursuits, rather than superficial small talk or social status games.

Overall, the assumption that sigma males are always introverted is a harmful stereotype that fails to capture the complexity and diversity of the personality type. While many sigma males may exhibit introverted tendencies, it is not a defining characteristic. Sigma males can be just as extroverted and socially adept as any other personality type, and should not be underestimated or dismissed based on assumptions and misconceptions.

7.8 The Sigma Male's Relationship with Money: Debunking the Stingy Stereotype

Sigma males are often perceived as stingy or cheap when it comes to money. This stereotype is often propagated by society, as well as by other personality types, who fail to understand the underlying reasons behind the sigma male's behavior. In reality, sigma males have a unique and complex relationship with money that is driven by their independent thinking, self-reliance, and desire for financial freedom.

At its core, the sigma male's relationship with money is based on the fundamental principle of self-reliance. Sigma males are fiercely independent individuals who value their autonomy and freedom above all else. They have a natural aversion to dependence on others, including financial dependence. This is why sigma males are often highly motivated to achieve financial independence at an early age, often by creating their own businesses or pursuing unconventional career paths.

One of the ways sigma males achieve financial independence is by adopting a frugal lifestyle. Contrary to popular belief, frugality does not imply stinginess or cheapness. Rather, frugality is the conscious decision to spend money on things that matter most and to cut back on unnecessary expenses. Sigma males are highly selective about their spending habits and prioritize investments that offer long-term benefits rather than short-term gratification.

Another reason why sigma males are often perceived as stingy is that they are highly skeptical of traditional financial systems and institutions. Sigma males are often critical of the mainstream financial advice dispensed by banks, financial advisors, and other conventional sources of financial wisdom. They are highly skeptical of the conventional wisdom that advocates for high levels of debt and reliance on the stock market. This skepticism is rooted in the sigma male's desire for financial independence and their desire to be in control of their own financial destiny.

Sigma males are also highly attuned to the concept of value. They understand that money is a finite resource, and they are always looking for ways to optimize their spending to get the most value for their money. This means that sigma males are highly selective about the products and services they purchase, and they often research extensively before making a purchase. Sigma males are highly analytical and logical, and they are always looking for ways to maximize their return on investment.

In addition to their frugality, sigma males also have a unique relationship with debt. While most people view debt as a necessary evil, sigma males view it as a tool that can be leveraged to achieve financial independence. Sigma males are highly strategic when it comes to taking on debt, and they are highly selective about the types of debt they pursue. They view debt as a means to an end, rather than an end in itself, and they are highly disciplined in their approach to debt management.

Another reason why sigma males are often perceived as stingy is that they are highly selective about the people they choose to share their wealth with. Sigma males are highly independent and self-reliant, and they do not like to rely on others for financial support. However, this does not mean that they are unwilling to share their wealth with others. Rather, sigma males are highly selective about the people they choose to support financially. They are highly attuned to the concept of reciprocity and are only willing to support those who are willing to reciprocate their generosity.

In conclusion, the stereotype that sigma males are stingy or cheap is a gross misrepresentation of their unique and complex relationship with money. Sigma males are highly independent, self-reliant individuals who value financial freedom above all else. They are highly selective about their spending habits, prioritize investments that offer long-term benefits, and are highly strategic when it comes to debt management. Sigma males are highly analytical and logical, and they are always looking for ways to optimize their spending to get the most value for their money. Rather than being stingy or cheap, sigma males are highly intentional about their financial decisions and are always looking for ways to achieve financial independence on their own terms.

7.9 The Importance of Understanding the Nuances of Sigma Male Personality Types.

The Sigma Male is a relatively new concept in the world of personality types. Unlike the Alpha Male, the Sigma Male is not interested in dominance or control, but rather in individualism and independence. They are often misunderstood and stereotyped as loners, misanthropes, or even asocial. However, these misconceptions are far from the truth. A deeper understanding of the Sigma Male personality type is essential to appreciate their unique qualities, and why they are an important part of our society.

At the heart of the Sigma Male personality type is a strong sense of independence. These men do not follow the pack, and they do not seek validation from others. Instead, they chart their own course in life, guided by their own principles and values. This independence can sometimes be perceived as aloofness or arrogance, but in reality, it is simply a reflection of their strong sense of self. They are self-sufficient and rely on their own abilities to navigate through life.

The importance of understanding the nuances of Sigma Male personality types lies in the fact that they are a valuable part of our society. Sigma Males are often highly intelligent, creative, and innovative. They are not afraid to challenge the status quo, and they can often see solutions to problems that others cannot. This makes them valuable contributors to fields such as science, technology, and the arts. They are also highly adaptable, able to thrive in environments that others may find challenging.

Unfortunately, society often misunderstands Sigma Males, and their unique qualities are often overlooked or undervalued. This is partly due to the fact that Sigma Males are not interested in seeking attention or validation from others. They do not fit into the traditional Alpha Male or Beta Male categories, which can make them difficult to categorize. However, it is important to recognize that Sigma Males have their own unique strengths and contributions to make.

One of the biggest misconceptions about Sigma Males is that they are antisocial or misanthropic. While it is true that they value their independence and autonomy, this does not mean that they are not capable of forming meaningful relationships. In fact, Sigma Males often have deep, meaningful connections with a select few individuals. They value quality over quantity when it comes to their relationships, and they are fiercely loyal to those they care about.

Another misconception about Sigma Males is that they lack ambition or drive. This is far from the truth. Sigma Males are highly motivated individuals, but their motivation comes from within rather than from external sources. They are not interested in climbing the corporate ladder or accumulating material possessions. Instead, they are driven by a desire to live a fulfilling life on their own terms. This often means pursuing their passions and interests, rather than conforming to societal expectations.

Understanding the nuances of Sigma Male personality types is essential for creating a more inclusive and accepting society. By recognizing the unique qualities and strengths of Sigma Males, we can better appreciate their contributions to our communities. We can also create environments that are more accommodating to their needs and preferences.

One area where this is particularly important is in the workplace. Sigma Males often do not thrive in traditional corporate environments, which can be hierarchical and focused on conformity. Instead, they may prefer more flexible work arrangements, such as freelancing or entrepreneurship. By recognizing and accommodating these preferences, employers can attract and retain talented Sigma Males, and create a more diverse and innovative workforce.

In addition to workplace accommodations, it is also important to recognize and address the stigma and stereotypes that surround Sigma Males. This can be done through education and awareness-raising campaigns. By dispelling the myths and misconceptions surrounding Sigma Males, we can create a more accepting and tolerant society.

In conclusion, the importance of understanding the nuances of Sigma Male personality types cannot be overstated. These men are often misunderstood and stereotyped, but they have their own unique strengths and contributions to make. By recognizing and appreciating these qualities, we can create a more inclusive and accepting society, and ensure that Sigma Males are valued and respected for who they are.

8. The Future of the Sigma Male: Trends and Predictions

8.1 The Sigma Male's Impact on Society

The Sigma Male's Impact on Society

The Sigma Male has been an elusive figure in society for years, often misunderstood and overlooked. However, the impact of the Sigma Male on society is undeniable. They possess many qualities that benefit society in various ways. In this chapter, we will explore the contributions of Sigma Males and the impact they have on society.

Sigma Males are unique individuals who value independence, creativity, and self-sufficiency. They are often introverted, but they are not shy or afraid to speak their minds. Sigma Males tend to be independent thinkers who don't conform to societal norms or follow trends blindly. They are not interested in seeking approval or validation from others, but rather in doing what they believe is right. This mindset results in a unique perspective that contributes to society in various ways.

Sigma Males are often leaders in their fields, whether it is in science, technology, or the arts. Their independent nature allows them to approach problems and challenges in unconventional ways, leading to new and innovative solutions. They are not afraid to take risks and pursue their ideas, even if they go against the status quo. This mindset has led to many significant breakthroughs and advancements in various fields.

In the business world, Sigma Males are often entrepreneurs, starting their own businesses and creating jobs for others. They tend to be self-sufficient and have a strong work ethic, which allows them to succeed even in challenging environments. Sigma Males are not interested in climbing the corporate ladder or seeking promotions; instead, they prefer to work on their own terms. This mentality has resulted in the creation of numerous successful businesses that have contributed to the economy and provided employment opportunities for many people.

The impact of Sigma Males is not limited to the workplace or the economy. They also play a significant role in shaping social and cultural trends. Sigma Males tend to be trendsetters rather than followers, creating new and exciting trends that influence fashion, music, and art. Their independent thinking and creativity often result in new and exciting ideas that challenge the status quo.

Sigma Males also value authenticity and honesty, which can have a positive impact on society. They are not interested in putting on a facade or pretending to be something they are not. They value genuine connections with others and tend to form deep, meaningful relationships. This mindset can lead to more authentic and honest interactions, which can improve communication and understanding between people.

Another significant impact of Sigma Males on society is their ability to challenge the status quo and push for change. They are not satisfied with the way things are and are always looking for ways to improve them. Sigma Males are often activists, fighting for causes they believe in and advocating for change. This mentality has led to many significant social and political movements throughout history.

Despite their many contributions to society, Sigma Males often face challenges and obstacles. They are often misunderstood and undervalued, and their independence can make it difficult for them to fit into traditional social structures. However, as society continues to evolve and become more accepting of individual differences, the impact of Sigma Males is likely to grow.

In conclusion, the impact of Sigma Males on society is significant and far-reaching. Their unique perspective and independent nature have led to many significant advancements and breakthroughs in various fields. They are often leaders in their fields, entrepreneurs, trendsetters, and activists. Their contributions have improved many aspects of society, including the economy, social and cultural trends, and political movements. Although they face many challenges, their impact on society is likely to continue to grow as society becomes more accepting of individual differences.

8.2 Technological Advancements and the Sigma Male

Technological advancements have changed the world, and in particular, they have changed the way Sigma males navigate it. The Sigma male is a lone wolf who values his independence, and technology has enabled him to maintain his autonomy while still being connected to the rest of the world. In this chapter, we will explore how technological advancements have impacted the Sigma male, and what trends and predictions we can make about the Sigma male's relationship with technology in the future.

One of the most significant technological advancements that has impacted the Sigma male is the internet. The internet has enabled Sigma males to connect with like-minded individuals from around the world, without having to leave their homes. This has been particularly beneficial for Sigma males who live in rural areas, where it may be challenging to find people with similar interests. The internet has also provided Sigma males with a platform to express themselves, whether that be through writing, creating art, or sharing their thoughts on social media platforms.

Another technological advancement that has impacted the Sigma male is the rise of remote work. Remote work has become increasingly popular in recent years, and it has provided Sigma males with the opportunity to work from anywhere in the world. This has given Sigma males the flexibility to work on their own terms, without having to conform to the norms of traditional office environments. Remote work has also enabled Sigma males to pursue their passions, whether that be traveling, pursuing hobbies, or spending time with family and friends.

Social media platforms have also impacted the Sigma male, and in particular, they have changed the way Sigma males communicate with others. Social media platforms have provided Sigma males with a way to connect with people they may not have had the opportunity to meet in person. This has been particularly beneficial for Sigma males who struggle with social anxiety or who find it challenging to meet new people. Social media platforms have also provided Sigma males with a platform to share their thoughts and ideas with a wider audience, which has enabled them to gain recognition and build communities around their interests.

Virtual reality (VR) is another technological advancement that has the potential to impact the Sigma male in the future. VR has the potential to provide a new level of immersion in media and entertainment, and it could enable Sigma males to create their own virtual worlds. This would provide Sigma males with a new level of autonomy, allowing them to create and explore their own unique environments without having to rely on the physical world. Furthermore, VR could provide Sigma males with the ability to connect with others in virtual spaces, enabling them to form communities and socialize with others without having to leave their homes.

Artificial intelligence (AI) is another technological advancement that could impact the Sigma male in the future. AI has the potential to automate many tasks, which could provide Sigma males with even more flexibility and autonomy in their lives. For example, AI could automate tasks such as scheduling appointments, managing finances, and even cooking meals. This would provide Sigma males with more time to pursue their passions and interests, without having to worry about mundane tasks.

The emergence of blockchain technology is another technological advancement that could impact the Sigma male in the future. Blockchain technology has the potential to provide a new level of security and privacy, which is essential for Sigma males who value their independence. Blockchain technology could provide Sigma males with a way to secure their personal information, financial transactions, and other sensitive data without having to rely on centralized institutions. This would give Sigma males more control over their data and enable them to maintain their privacy and independence.

In conclusion, technological advancements have had a significant impact on the Sigma male, and they will continue to do so in the future. The internet has provided Sigma males with a platform to connect with others and express themselves, while remote work and social media have provided Sigma males with more flexibility and autonomy in their lives. VR, AI, and blockchain technology are all technological advancements that have the potential to impact the Sigma male in the future, providing them with even more autonomy and independence. As technology continues to evolve, it will be interesting to see how Sigma males navigate these changes and continue to maintain their independence and autonomy.

8.3 The Rise of Entrepreneurial Sigma Males

The Sigma Male has traditionally been seen as the lone wolf, the outsider who prefers to stay away from the social norms and expectations. However, with the rise of the entrepreneurial spirit, there has been a new type of Sigma Male emerging- the Entrepreneurial Sigma Male. This new breed of Sigma Male is not only independent, but also driven, ambitious, and keen to build their own empire.

The Entrepreneurial Sigma Male has a unique set of characteristics that distinguish them from other types of entrepreneurs. They are often introverted and enjoy working alone, but they possess a strong sense of self-confidence and a willingness to take risks. They are also highly adaptable and creative, able to see opportunities where others may not.

These traits make them ideal candidates for entrepreneurship, as they possess the drive and focus required to succeed in a competitive market. They are able to create their own path, without relying on the approval of others, and are not afraid to take bold risks to achieve their goals.

One of the most important characteristics of the Entrepreneurial Sigma Male is their ability to think outside of the box. They are not constrained by traditional ways of doing things, and are willing to take risks and try new things. They are constantly seeking out new opportunities, and are not afraid to pivot or change direction if things are not working out.

The Entrepreneurial Sigma Male is also highly independent, and values their freedom and autonomy above all else. They are not interested in working for someone else or following someone else's vision. Instead, they want to be their own boss, and create their own opportunities. This independence can sometimes be mistaken for arrogance or aloofness, but it is simply a reflection of their desire to chart their own path.

Another key trait of the Entrepreneurial Sigma Male is their ability to focus and prioritize. They are often laser-focused on their goals, and are able to block out distractions and stay committed to their vision. They are also excellent at prioritizing their time and resources, and are able to identify the most important tasks and activities that will help them achieve their goals.

One of the most impressive things about the Entrepreneurial Sigma Male is their resilience and perseverance. Starting a business can be incredibly challenging, and there will inevitably be setbacks and failures along the way. However, the Entrepreneurial Sigma Male is able to bounce back from these setbacks, learn from their mistakes, and keep moving forward. They have a strong sense of self-belief, and are not deterred by failure.

The rise of the Entrepreneurial Sigma Male has been driven by a number of factors. The first is the changing nature of work and employment. Many people are now looking for more flexibility and autonomy in their work, and are turning to entrepreneurship as a way to achieve this. The rise of the gig economy and the increasing number of freelance opportunities means that it is now easier than ever to start a business and work for yourself.

Another factor driving the rise of the Entrepreneurial Sigma Male is the changing cultural attitudes towards entrepreneurship. In the past, starting a business was seen as risky and unconventional. However, in recent years, entrepreneurship has become much more mainstream and accepted. It is now seen as a legitimate career path, and there is a wealth of resources and support available to help entrepreneurs get started.

The rise of social media and online platforms has also played a role in the rise of the Entrepreneurial Sigma Male. These platforms have made it easier than ever to connect with potential customers and clients, and to build a brand and a following. They have also made it possible to start a business with very little capital or resources, as many online businesses can be started from the comfort of your own home.

Overall, the rise of the Entrepreneurial Sigma Male is a positive trend for the business world. These individuals are bringing a fresh perspective and a new set of skills to the table, and are helping to drive innovation and growth. They are also helping to break down traditional barriers and norms, and are paving the way for a new generation of independent, creative, and successful entrepreneurs.

8.4 Globalization and the Sigma Male

Globalization has had a significant impact on the Sigma Male, as it has on many other aspects of our society. With the world becoming more interconnected and technology advancing at a rapid pace, the Sigma Male has been forced to adapt to new ways of living, working, and socializing.

The Sigma Male is often characterized as an independent and self-reliant individual who values his freedom and autonomy above all else. In many ways, globalization has played into these strengths by providing the Sigma Male with more opportunities to live and work on his own terms. With the rise of remote work and digital nomadism, the Sigma Male who once felt trapped in traditional office environments can now work from anywhere in the world.

However, globalization has also brought with it some challenges for the Sigma Male. The increasing pace of change and uncertainty in today's world can be overwhelming, and the Sigma Male may struggle to keep up with the constantly shifting landscape. The globalization of the economy has also made it more difficult for the Sigma Male to find stable and secure work, as jobs are outsourced and companies are constantly restructuring to stay competitive.

Additionally, globalization has brought with it a more interconnected and interdependent world, which can be difficult for the Sigma Male who values his independence and self-sufficiency. The Sigma Male may feel that he is losing control over his life as he is increasingly influenced by global trends and events outside of his control.

Despite these challenges, the Sigma Male has the potential to thrive in a globalized world. His self-reliance, adaptability, and resourcefulness are valuable qualities in a world that is constantly changing and evolving. The Sigma Male's ability to think outside of the box and find creative solutions to problems can also be an asset in a globalized economy where innovation is key.

Furthermore, the Sigma Male's distaste for conformity and groupthink can be especially valuable in a world where conformity is often rewarded at the expense of independent thought. The Sigma Male's willingness to challenge conventional wisdom and think for himself can be a powerful force for change and progress in a globalized society.

In order to navigate the challenges of globalization, the Sigma Male must continue to develop his skills and stay on top of industry trends and technological advancements. He must also be willing to adapt to new ways of living and working, as traditional career paths become less stable and predictable.

One way that the Sigma Male can thrive in a globalized world is by cultivating his network of contacts and building strong relationships with others in his field. The Sigma Male may be independent, but he is not an island. By building a strong network of colleagues and mentors, he can stay up-to-date on industry developments and gain valuable insights into new opportunities.

Another way that the Sigma Male can thrive in a globalized world is by staying true to his values and maintaining his independence. The Sigma Male must resist the pressure to conform to societal norms and expectations, and instead stay focused on his own goals and priorities. By staying true to himself, the Sigma Male can maintain his sense of autonomy and self-reliance, even in a world that is increasingly interconnected and interdependent.

In conclusion, globalization has had both positive and negative impacts on the Sigma Male. While it has provided him with more opportunities to live and work on his own terms, it has also brought with it new challenges and uncertainties. However, with his independent spirit, adaptability, and resourcefulness, the Sigma Male has the potential to thrive in a globalized world. By staying true to his values and continuing to develop his skills and networks, the Sigma Male can navigate the challenges of globalization and emerge as a leader and innovator in his field.

8.5 The Sigma Male in Politics and Leadership

The Sigma Male has always been a bit of an enigma, operating outside of traditional social hierarchies and power structures. As a result, the Sigma Male has not been well represented in politics and leadership roles historically. However, in recent years, there has been a growing interest in the Sigma Male as a potential force for change in these fields.

Part of the reason for this interest is the changing landscape of politics and leadership. The traditional alpha male archetype, which has long dominated these fields, is facing increasing scrutiny and criticism. The alpha male is often seen as aggressive, domineering, and insensitive, traits that are not well-suited to the complex and nuanced world of modern politics and leadership. Additionally, the alpha male's tendency to prioritize personal ambition over the collective good can be counterproductive in these roles.

The Sigma Male, on the other hand, possesses many traits that are well-suited to politics and leadership. For one, the Sigma Male is highly independent and self-reliant. This makes them less susceptible to pressure from special interest groups or party leaders, and more likely to make decisions based on their own convictions and principles. This is an important trait in a world where politicians and leaders are often seen as being beholden to lobbyists, donors, and other outside interests.

Another key trait of the Sigma Male that makes them well-suited to politics and leadership is their ability to think critically and independently. The Sigma Male is not swayed by conventional wisdom or groupthink, instead preferring to analyze issues on their own and come to their own conclusions. This is an important trait in a world where politicians and leaders are often criticized for being too beholden to their party or ideology.

In addition to these traits, the Sigma Male also possesses a number of other qualities that are well-suited to leadership and politics. For one, they tend to be highly adaptable and able to thrive in diverse environments. This makes them well-suited to the fast-paced and constantly changing world of politics and leadership. Additionally, the Sigma Male is often highly intelligent and capable of processing complex information quickly and effectively. This is an important trait in a world where decisions must often be made quickly and with incomplete information.

Despite these qualities, the Sigma Male still faces a number of challenges when it comes to politics and leadership. For one, they often struggle with networking and building relationships, which are important skills in these fields. Additionally, the Sigma Male's independent streak can sometimes be seen as a liability, making it difficult for them to work effectively with others and build coalitions.

Despite these challenges, there are some signs that the Sigma Male may be starting to make their mark in politics and leadership. One example is the rise of independent politicians, who are often seen as embodying many of the traits of the Sigma Male. These politicians often eschew traditional party affiliations and instead focus on issues and ideas that resonate with their constituents.

Another example is the growing interest in leadership models that prioritize collaboration, empathy, and emotional intelligence. These models are often seen as more compatible with the traits of the Sigma Male than the traditional alpha male model of leadership.

Overall, the Sigma Male has the potential to be a powerful force for change in politics and leadership. Their independence, critical thinking skills, and adaptability make them well-suited to the complex and rapidly evolving world of these fields. However, they will need to overcome certain challenges and develop key skills, such as networking and relationship-building, in order to fully realize their potential. As the world continues to evolve and the traditional alpha male archetype comes under increasing scrutiny, the Sigma Male may find themselves in a position to reshape politics and leadership in their own image.

8.6 The Future of Male Identity: Sigma vs Alpha

In the global society, the concept of masculinity has undergone a significant shift in recent times. Men are becoming more aware of the different paths they can take to achieve success, and the traditional notion of what it means to be an alpha male no longer resonates with everyone. Instead, men are beginning to carve out a new identity for themselves - one that is more independent, more self-directed, and less concerned with external validation. This new identity is known as the Sigma male, and it represents a paradigm shift in how men view their place in the world.

But as the Sigma male identity grows in popularity, a new debate is emerging within male circles: what is the future of male identity? Will the Sigma male identity continue to grow and thrive, or will it eventually be replaced by a new iteration of the alpha male? And what are the main differences between these two identities? In this chapter, we will explore the future of male identity by examining the Sigma male and the alpha male, and comparing the two in terms of their values, beliefs, and behaviors.

The Sigma Male

The Sigma male is a relatively new concept, and it has only recently gained traction in mainstream consciousness. The Sigma male is often described as an independent, introverted, and introspective type of man who values autonomy, freedom, and self-development above all else. Unlike the alpha male, who is more focused on dominating others and seeking external validation, the Sigma male is more concerned with his own personal growth and development.

He is often seen as a lone wolf, someone who operates on the fringes of society and does not conform to traditional societal norms.

One of the defining characteristics of the Sigma male is his ability to operate independently, without relying on others for support or validation. This independence can be seen in his work life, where he often prefers to work on his own projects rather than collaborating with others. Similarly, in his personal life, he may prefer to spend time alone rather than in large social groups. This independence does not mean that the Sigma male is anti-social, however. Instead, he values his relationships with others on a deeper level, preferring to cultivate a small circle of close friends rather than a large group of acquaintances.

Another defining characteristic of the Sigma male is his focus on personal development. He is always seeking to improve himself in some way, whether it is through learning new skills or expanding his knowledge base. This focus on self-improvement is often driven by a desire to achieve personal fulfillment rather than external validation from others. The Sigma male is constantly pushing himself to be the best version of himself, and he is not afraid to take risks or pursue his passions, even if it means going against the norm.

The Alpha Male

The alpha male, on the other hand, is a more traditional type of man who is focused on dominating others and achieving external validation. The alpha male is often seen as the archetypal male, the one who is strong, confident, and aggressive. He is the leader of the pack, the one who sets the rules and dictates the terms of engagement. Unlike the Sigma male, who is more focused on personal growth and development, the alpha male is more concerned with achieving power and status within his social group.

One of the defining characteristics of the alpha male is his focus on dominance. He is always seeking to assert his dominance over others, whether it is in the workplace, in social situations, or in his personal life. This focus on dominance is often driven by a desire to achieve external validation from others, such as respect, admiration, or fear. The alpha male is not afraid to use his physical or social power to achieve his goals, and he is often seen as a force to be reckoned with.

Another defining characteristic of the alpha male is his focus on social status. He is always seeking to climb the social ladder, whether it is in his work life, his personal life, or his romantic relationships. The alpha male is often driven by a desire to be seen as the most successful or powerful person in the room, and he is not afraid to manipulate or dominate others to achieve this goal. This focus on social status can sometimes be at odds with the alpha male's personal values or goals, as he may prioritize external validation over personal fulfillment.

Sigma vs Alpha: The Future of Male Identity

So what does the future hold for male identity? Will the Sigma male continue to grow in popularity, or will the alpha male stage a comeback? There is no clear answer to these questions, as both identities have their own strengths and weaknesses. However, it is clear that the Sigma male represents a new paradigm in male identity, one that is more focused on personal growth and development rather than external validation.

One of the main reasons why the Sigma male is gaining popularity is that it resonates with many men who feel that the traditional alpha male identity is too constraining. The Sigma male offers an alternative path to success, one that is less focused on dominating others and more focused on personal fulfillment. This new identity appeals to men who value autonomy, freedom, and self-direction, and who are not afraid to go against the norm.

Another reason why the Sigma male is gaining popularity is that it reflects the changing nature of society. In a world that is becoming more complex and interconnected, the traditional alpha male identity may no longer be sufficient. Instead, men are beginning to recognize the importance of self-reflection, personal growth, and emotional intelligence. The Sigma male embodies these values, and he represents a new way of navigating the world.

However, it is important to note that the alpha male identity is not going away anytime soon. There will always be men who value dominance, power, and external validation, and who are willing to use their physical or social power to achieve their goals. The alpha male identity will continue to be relevant for these men, and it will likely continue to hold sway in certain domains, such as politics or business.

In conclusion, the future of male identity is complex and multifaceted. The Sigma male represents a new paradigm in male identity, one that is more focused on personal growth and development rather than external validation. However, the alpha male identity will likely continue to hold sway in certain domains, and there will always be men who value dominance, power, and external validation. Ultimately, the future of male identity will be determined by the choices and actions of individual men, as they navigate the changing landscape of society and forge their own path to success and fulfillment.

8.7 The Importance of Emotional Intelligence for Sigma Males

In recent years, there has been a growing conversation about emotional intelligence and its importance in personal and professional success. Emotional intelligence refers to a person's ability to recognize and manage their own emotions, as well as understand and empathize with the emotions of others. While traditionally associated with more socially-oriented personality types, emotional intelligence is increasingly recognized as a crucial trait for independent and introverted individuals as well. In particular, sigma males, who are known for their independent and self-sufficient nature, can greatly benefit from cultivating emotional intelligence.

One of the key reasons why emotional intelligence is important for sigma males is that it helps them build stronger relationships with others. While sigma males may value their independence, they still need people in their lives - whether it's for friendship, romance, or professional networking. However, because sigma males tend to be more reserved and private, they may struggle to form connections with others. This is where emotional intelligence comes in. By learning to recognize and manage their own emotions, sigma males can become more self-aware and therefore more able to communicate their needs and feelings to others. Additionally, by developing empathy and understanding for the emotions of others, sigma males can become better listeners and more effective communicators. This, in turn, can help them build more meaningful and fulfilling relationships with others.

Another reason why emotional intelligence is important for sigma males is that it can help them navigate conflict and difficult situations. Sigma males tend to be independent and self-sufficient, but that doesn't mean they never encounter challenges or obstacles. In fact, because sigma males often march to the beat of their own drum, they may face more resistance or pushback from others than more conformist personality types. In these situations, emotional intelligence can be a valuable tool for managing emotions and finding solutions. For example, a sigma male with strong emotional intelligence might be able to recognize when they're feeling defensive or angry during a confrontation, and take steps to calm themselves down and approach the situation more rationally. They might also be better equipped to find common ground with others and work towards a mutually beneficial resolution.

Additionally, emotional intelligence can help sigma males succeed in the workplace. Many sigma males are entrepreneurs, freelancers, or independent contractors, and therefore need to be able to work effectively with clients, collaborators, and other stakeholders. Emotional intelligence can help them build trust, communicate clearly, and navigate difficult conversations with clients or colleagues. It can also help them manage stress and burnout, which can be common challenges for independent workers who need to manage their own schedules and workload. By recognizing their own emotions and finding healthy ways to cope with stress, sigma males can stay productive and focused on their goals.

Overall, emotional intelligence is an essential trait for sigma males who want to succeed in their personal and professional lives. By learning to recognize and manage their own emotions, as well as understand and empathize with the emotions of others, sigma males can build stronger relationships, navigate conflict and difficult situations, and achieve their goals with confidence and resilience. While emotional intelligence may not come as naturally to sigma males as it does to more socially-oriented personality types, it is a skill that can be learned and cultivated with practice. Whether through therapy, mindfulness practices, or simply reflecting on their own emotions and behaviors, sigma males can take steps to develop their emotional intelligence and become more successful and fulfilled in all areas of their lives.

8.8 The Role of Mentorship in the Development of Sigma Males

The role of mentorship in the development of Sigma Males is crucial as it helps them navigate through the complexities of life and gain a better understanding of the world. As Sigma Males are independent and self-reliant by nature, they tend to shy away from seeking help or guidance from others. However, mentorship provides a platform for them to learn from someone who has more experience and expertise in their chosen field or area of interest.

Mentors can provide valuable insights and advice on how to navigate through challenging situations, make better decisions, and achieve personal and professional goals. They can also help Sigma Males identify their strengths and weaknesses, and provide guidance on how to leverage their strengths and improve on their weaknesses. A mentor can be a sounding board for new ideas and provide honest feedback on their protégé's progress.

One of the most significant benefits of mentorship is that it helps Sigma Males build a professional network. A mentor can introduce them to other professionals in their field, which can be valuable for networking and career growth opportunities. By building a network of contacts, Sigma Males can expand their knowledge and learn about new opportunities in their industry.

Mentorship can also help Sigma Males develop valuable soft skills like communication, leadership, and teamwork. These skills are essential for success in any profession, and a mentor can provide guidance on how to improve them. By developing these skills, Sigma Males can become more effective communicators, better leaders, and more collaborative team members.

Another benefit of mentorship is that it can help Sigma Males avoid common mistakes and pitfalls. Mentors can provide guidance on how to avoid common pitfalls and mistakes that they themselves may have experienced. By learning from their mentor's mistakes, Sigma Males can avoid making the same mistakes themselves, which can save them time, money, and frustration.

Mentorship can also help Sigma Males develop a growth mindset. A growth mindset is the belief that one can learn, grow, and improve through hard work and dedication. A mentor can help instill this mindset in their protégé by encouraging them to take risks, embrace challenges, and learn from failures. By developing a growth mindset, Sigma Males can become more resilient and adaptable, which are essential traits for success in any field.

In addition to professional mentorship, Sigma Males can also benefit from personal mentorship. A personal mentor can provide guidance on how to navigate through personal challenges and develop a more fulfilling life. Personal mentorship can help Sigma Males develop their emotional intelligence, build stronger relationships, and find a better work-life balance.

In conclusion, mentorship plays a vital role in the development of Sigma Males. It provides a platform for them to learn from someone who has more experience and expertise in their chosen field or area of interest. It can help them build a professional network, develop valuable soft skills, avoid common mistakes and pitfalls, and develop a growth mindset. Personal mentorship can also help Sigma Males develop their emotional intelligence, build stronger relationships, and find a better work-life balance. Mentorship is an essential tool for the development of Sigma Males, and it should be embraced as a valuable resource for personal and professional growth.

8.9 The Sigma Male and the Pursuit of Happiness

The pursuit of happiness is a fundamental human right and one that has been the focus of many scholars and philosophers throughout history. It is a concept that can be defined in many ways, but ultimately, it refers to the feeling of contentment and satisfaction that comes from living a fulfilling life. For the Sigma Male, the pursuit of happiness is particularly important, as it is often the driving force behind their independent nature and desire to live life on their own terms.

One of the defining characteristics of the Sigma Male is their desire for freedom and autonomy. Unlike the Alpha Male, who seeks power and control over others, or the Beta Male, who seeks acceptance and belonging within a group, the Sigma Male values their independence above all else. They are often seen as outsiders, rebels, or non-conformists, and are more likely to forge their own path in life rather than following the traditional societal norms.

This desire for independence means that the pursuit of happiness for the Sigma Male is often centered around achieving personal fulfillment and finding their own sense of purpose. They are not content to simply follow in the footsteps of others or conform to societal expectations, but instead seek out experiences and opportunities that align with their own values and beliefs.

One way that the Sigma Male pursues happiness is through their career choices. Unlike the Alpha Male, who may be motivated by status and prestige, the Sigma Male is more likely to choose a career based on their personal interests and passions. They may be drawn to more unconventional fields, such as art, music, or entrepreneurship, where they can use their creativity and independent spirit to achieve success on their own terms.

Another way that the Sigma Male pursues happiness is through their relationships. While they may not be as concerned with social status or popularity as the Alpha Male or Beta Male, they still value meaningful connections with others. However, they may approach relationships in a more reserved or cautious manner, preferring to keep a certain level of distance and independence rather than becoming too emotionally dependent on others.

Overall, the pursuit of happiness for the Sigma Male is a deeply personal and individual journey. They are not content to simply follow the crowd or conform to societal norms, but instead seek out their own path in life. Whether it is through their career, relationships, or personal interests, the Sigma Male is always striving to find their own sense of fulfillment and happiness.

9. Becoming a Sigma Male: Steps to Independence and Self-Discovery

9.1 Defining Your Values and Priorities

To become a Sigma Male, it is essential to have a clear understanding of your values and priorities. In essence, your values are the things that matter most to you and guide your behavior, while your priorities are the areas of your life that take precedence over others. Without a clear understanding of your values and priorities, it is easy to get lost in the chaos of life and lose sight of what truly matters.

The first step in defining your values is to take a step back and reflect on what is most important to you. This could include things like honesty, integrity, loyalty, independence, and self-reliance. It is important to be honest with yourself and determine what truly matters to you, as opposed to what you think should matter or what others say should matter.

Once you have a clear understanding of your values, it is important to live your life in accordance with them. This means making decisions that align with your values, even if they are not the most popular or convenient choices. For example, if one of your values is honesty, you should always strive to tell the truth, even if it is difficult or uncomfortable.

In addition to defining your values, it is important to prioritize the areas of your life that are most important to you. This could include things like family, career, health, and personal growth. Prioritizing your life allows you to focus your time and energy on the things that matter most, rather than getting bogged down by distractions and things that do not align with your values.

To prioritize your life, it is important to determine what areas of your life are most important to you and allocate your time and resources accordingly. For example, if family is a top priority, you may choose to spend more time with your loved ones and make sacrifices in other areas of your life to ensure that you are able to maintain strong relationships with those closest to you.

Another important aspect of defining your values and priorities is being able to say no to things that do not align with them. This can be difficult, especially if you are used to saying yes to everything or feel pressure from others to conform to their expectations. However, being able to say no when necessary is a critical skill for living a fulfilling and authentic life.

In order to say no effectively, it is important to be clear and concise in your communication. Let others know that you value their opinions and appreciate their invitations, but that you are unable to participate at this time. It is also important to remain firm in your decision and not be swayed by guilt or pressure from others.

Defining your values and priorities is an ongoing process, as your values may change over time in response to new experiences and insights. It is important to regularly reflect on your values and priorities and make adjustments as necessary to ensure that you are living a life that is true to who you are.

In conclusion, defining your values and priorities is a critical step in becoming a Sigma Male. By having a clear understanding of what matters most to you and prioritizing the areas of your life that are most important, you are better able to navigate the complexities of life and live according to your own unique vision. Take the time to reflect on your values and priorities, and make the necessary changes to align your life with what truly matters to you.

9.2 Developing a Strong Sense of Self

One of the key traits of a sigma male is their strong sense of self, a deep understanding of who they are and what they stand for. This sense of self is not something that comes naturally to everyone, and it often takes time and effort to develop. However, it is an essential part of becoming a sigma male, as it allows you to navigate the world with confidence and conviction, staying true to your values and goals.

There are several steps you can take to develop a strong sense of self, including:

1. Self-Reflection

The first step to developing a strong sense of self is to take the time to reflect on your values, beliefs, and goals. This involves looking inward and examining your thoughts, feelings, and behaviors to gain a deeper understanding of who you are.

Ask yourself questions like:

- What do I value most in life?
- What are my strengths and weaknesses?
- What motivates me?
- What are my long-term goals?
- What do I believe in?

By answering these questions, you can start to build a clear picture of who you are and what you stand for.

2. Define Your Boundaries

Once you have a clear understanding of your values and beliefs, it's important to set boundaries that align with them. Boundaries are essential for protecting your sense of self and ensuring that you are not compromising your values or goals for others.

Boundaries can include:

- Saying no to requests or demands that go against your values or goals
- Setting limits on the time and energy you give to others
- Communicating your needs and expectations in relationships
- Avoiding situations or people that make you feel uncomfortable or unhappy

By setting clear boundaries, you are sending a message to yourself and others that you value yourself and your goals, and you will not compromise them.

3. Practice Self-Acceptance

Another important aspect of developing a strong sense of self is practicing self-acceptance. This means accepting yourself for who you are, flaws and all. It's important to remember that nobody is perfect, and we all have areas where we can improve.

To practice self-acceptance, try:

- Celebrating your strengths and accomplishments
- Being kind and forgiving to yourself when you make mistakes
- Letting go of self-criticism and negative self-talk
- Focusing on your positive qualities and attributes

By accepting yourself for who you are, you are showing yourself love and respect, which can boost your self-esteem and confidence.

4. Seek Out New Experiences

One way to build a strong sense of self is to seek out new experiences and challenges. This can help you discover your strengths and weaknesses, as well as build your resilience and confidence.

New experiences can include:

- Trying a new hobby or activity
- Traveling to a new place
- Taking a class or workshop
- Volunteering in your community
- Meeting new people and making new friends

By pushing yourself out of your comfort zone and trying new things, you are expanding your horizons and discovering new aspects of yourself.

5. Set Clear Goals

Setting clear goals is another important aspect of developing a strong sense of self. By setting goals, you are giving yourself something to work towards and a sense of purpose.

When setting goals, make sure they are:

- Specific: Make sure your goals are clear and well-defined.
- Measurable: Ensure that you can track your progress and measure your success.
- Realistic: Set goals that are achievable and realistic for your current situation.
- Time-bound: Give yourself a deadline to work towards.

By setting clear goals, you are keeping yourself accountable and motivated, and you can track your progress towards achieving them.

In conclusion, developing a strong sense of self is essential for becoming a sigma male. By taking the time to reflect on your values, setting clear boundaries, practicing self-acceptance, seeking out new experiences, and setting clear goals, you can build a deep understanding of who you are and what you stand for. This sense of self can give you the confidence and conviction to navigate the world with independence and purpose, staying true to your values and goals.

9.3 Embracing Personal Growth and Learning

Self-improvement is one of the key elements of becoming a sigma male. Whether it is seeking new knowledge, developing a new skill or mastering a new approach to life, a sigma male seeks personal growth as a way of life. This is not something that happens overnight or without effort; it takes a conscious decision to embrace personal growth and learning as a way of life.

The first step in this journey is to acknowledge the importance of learning in your life. Many people believe that learning is something they do in school, and that once they are done, they can stop learning. This is far from the truth, as learning is a lifelong process that never ends. There is always something new to learn, no matter how old you are. Once you accept this fact, you will start to see the world with new eyes and be open to new opportunities to learn.

The next step is to identify the areas in which you want to grow. What skills do you want to master, what knowledge do you want to acquire? The areas can be personal, professional or academic. The important thing is that they are meaningful to you and that they will help you achieve your goals. Once you have identified the areas, you can start to develop a plan of action to achieve them.

The third step is to take action. It is not enough to have a plan; you need to take action to make it happen. This means committing to your plan and taking the necessary steps to achieve your goals. It may mean taking classes, reading books, attending workshops or seeking out mentors. Whatever it takes, you need to be willing to do it.

One of the most important aspects of personal growth and learning is to embrace failure. Failure is not something to be feared, but rather an opportunity to learn and grow. If you never fail, you will never learn, and you will never reach your full potential. Instead of fearing failure, embrace it as a natural part of the learning process. Learn from your mistakes and use them to improve your approach.

Another important aspect of personal growth and learning is to seek out feedback. Feedback is essential for growth as it can help you identify areas where you need to improve. This can come from mentors, colleagues, friends or family. Be open to feedback, even if it is negative, as it can help you grow and develop.

Finally, it is important to stay curious. A sigma male is always seeking out new knowledge and experiences. They are curious about the world and the people around them. This curiosity drives them to seek out new opportunities to learn and grow. Staying curious also helps you stay open-minded and flexible, which is essential in today's constantly changing world.

In conclusion, embracing personal growth and learning is essential for becoming a sigma male. It requires a conscious decision to make learning a way of life, a commitment to identify areas for growth, a willingness to take action, an openness to failure, a desire for feedback and a curiosity about the world. It is not always easy, but the rewards are significant. By embracing personal growth and learning, you will become a stronger, more confident and more independent person. You will be better equipped to navigate the world around you and to achieve your goals.

9.4 Building a Support System

Becoming a Sigma Male requires a great deal of independence and self-discovery, but that doesn't mean you have to go it alone. In fact, building a strong support system can be a key part of your journey towards independence and self-actualization. A support system can provide you with the emotional, practical, and social support you need to overcome challenges, pursue your goals, and cultivate a sense of purpose and fulfillment.

There are many different types of support systems you can build, depending on your individual needs and preferences. Here are some key areas to consider:

Cultivating Positive Relationships

One of the most important aspects of building a support system is cultivating positive relationships with people who share your values, interests, and goals. Whether it's a close friend, a romantic partner, or a group of like-minded individuals, having a social network that supports and encourages you can be a powerful force for change.

To cultivate positive relationships, start by identifying the people in your life who share your values and interests. Look for people who are positive, supportive, and open-minded, and who are willing to listen and offer feedback when you need it.

Once you've identified some potential allies, start investing time and energy into building those relationships. This might involve initiating conversations, scheduling social events, or simply spending more time together. Be sure to communicate your needs and expectations clearly, and be open to feedback and suggestions from others.

Finding a Mentor

Another important component of building a support system is finding a mentor who can offer guidance, advice, and support as you navigate the challenges of life. A mentor can be someone who has already achieved the goals you're striving for, or simply someone who has more experience and wisdom than you do.

To find a mentor, start by identifying people in your industry, community, or area of interest who have the skills and experience you admire. Reach out to these individuals and express your interest in learning from them. Be clear about your goals and aspirations, and be open to feedback and guidance.

Remember, finding a mentor is not just about what you can get from them; it's also about building a mutually beneficial relationship. Be willing to offer your own skills, knowledge, and experience in exchange for their guidance and support.

Building a Supportive Environment

In addition to cultivating positive relationships and finding a mentor, building a supportive environment can also be a key part of your support system. This might involve creating a physical environment that supports your goals and interests, such as a home office or a workout space, or it might involve finding a community or organization that shares your values and passions.

To build a supportive environment, start by identifying the physical and social spaces that make you feel most comfortable and inspired. This might involve creating a home office that's conducive to creativity and productivity, or finding a gym or workout class where you feel motivated and energized.

You can also build a supportive environment by seeking out communities or organizations that align with your values and interests. This might involve joining a social club, volunteering for a cause you believe in, or attending events and conferences related to your industry or area of interest.

Developing Self-Compassion

Finally, building a support system also requires developing self-compassion and self-care practices that help you stay grounded, centered, and resilient in the face of life's challenges. Self-compassion involves treating yourself with kindness and understanding, even when you make mistakes or face setbacks.

To develop self-compassion, start by paying attention to your inner critic and the negative self-talk that might be holding you back. Challenge these negative thoughts and replace them with positive affirmations and self-talk that reinforces your strengths and positive qualities.

You can also develop self-compassion by incorporating self-care practices into your daily routine. This might involve getting enough sleep, eating healthy foods, practicing mindfulness or meditation, or engaging in physical activity that makes you feel good.

Building a support system requires effort, intentionality, and a willingness to be vulnerable and open with others. But it can be a powerful force for change, helping you overcome challenges, pursue your goals, and cultivate a sense of purpose and fulfillment in your life.

9.5 Pursuing Your Passions and Interests

One of the key elements of becoming a Sigma Male is pursuing your passions and interests. Many men spend their lives doing what they think they are supposed to do, rather than what they truly want to do. This often leads to a feeling of dissatisfaction and unfulfillment. However, a Sigma Male understands that pursuing your passions and interests is integral to living a truly fulfilling life.

So, what exactly does it mean to pursue your passions and interests? It means taking the time to figure out what you truly enjoy doing and then actively pursuing those things. This can take many forms, from taking up a new hobby to starting your own business. The key is to find what truly excites and motivates you, and then devote your time and energy to it.

One of the benefits of pursuing your passions and interests is that it can lead to a sense of purpose and meaning in your life. When you are doing something that you truly enjoy, it can feel like you are contributing something valuable to the world. This can lead to a sense of fulfillment that is hard to find in other areas of life.

Another benefit of pursuing your passions and interests is that it can lead to personal growth and development. When you are doing something that you truly enjoy, you are more likely to put in the time and effort needed to get better at it. This can lead to a sense of accomplishment and pride in your abilities.

However, pursuing your passions and interests is not always easy. It can require a lot of hard work and dedication, and it may not always be financially or socially rewarding. This is why many men choose to ignore their passions and interests in favor of more practical pursuits. However, a Sigma Male understands that true happiness and fulfillment come from pursuing what you love, even if it is not always easy.

So, how can you go about pursuing your passions and interests? The first step is to take some time to figure out what you truly enjoy doing. This can be a difficult process, as many men have spent their lives doing what they think they are supposed to do, rather than what they truly want to do. However, it is important to take the time to really think about what you love doing, and what makes you feel passionate and motivated.

Once you have identified your passions and interests, it is important to start taking action to pursue them. This may mean taking a class, joining a club or group, or simply making time in your schedule to devote to your interests. The key is to start taking action and making progress towards your goals.

It is also important to remember that pursuing your passions and interests is a lifelong process. You may find that your interests change over time, or that you discover new passions as you go along. This is perfectly normal, and it is important to be open to new experiences and opportunities as they arise.

Ultimately, pursuing your passions and interests is a key component of becoming a Sigma Male. By doing what you love and following your own path, you can find true happiness, fulfillment, and independence in your life. So, take the time to identify your passions and interests, and then start taking action to pursue them. Your life will be all the richer for it.

9.6 Taking Risks and Embracing Failure

One of the key characteristics of a Sigma male is the willingness to take risks and embrace failure. Unlike traditional alpha males, who often seek to dominate and control their environment, Sigma males are more interested in exploring new opportunities and pushing the boundaries of what is possible. This can be seen in their approach to life, work, and relationships.

In order to understand why taking risks and embracing failure is so important for Sigma males, it is useful to explore the concept of risk itself. In essence, risk is the potential for loss or harm that comes with any decision or action. It can take many forms, from financial risks such as investing in a new business venture, to personal risks such as pursuing a romantic relationship with someone who may not feel the same way.

For many people, the idea of taking risks is inherently scary. This is because we are all wired to seek safety and security, both on a physical and emotional level. When faced with the possibility of losing something we value - whether that is our money, our reputation, or our sense of self-worth - our natural response is often to retreat and avoid taking any action that might put us in harm's way.

However, Sigma males understand that taking risks is often the only way to achieve greatness. Whether it is starting a new business, pursuing a passion project, or entering into a new relationship, there is always a degree of uncertainty and risk involved. But by embracing those risks and being willing to fail, Sigma males are able to push past their fear and achieve their goals.

Of course, this is not to say that Sigma males are reckless or irresponsible when it comes to risk-taking. On the contrary, they are often very calculated and deliberate in their approach, carefully weighing the potential benefits and drawbacks of any given decision. But when the potential reward is great enough, they are willing to take the plunge and see what happens.

One of the keys to successful risk-taking is learning how to embrace failure. For many people, the fear of failure is the biggest obstacle to taking risks and pursuing their dreams. But Sigma males understand that failure is not the end of the world - in fact, it can often be a valuable learning experience.

When we fail at something, whether it is a business venture or a relationship, we are forced to confront our mistakes and weaknesses. We are forced to reevaluate our approach and figure out what went wrong. This can be a painful and humbling process, but it is also incredibly valuable. By learning from our failures, we can become stronger, wiser, and more resilient.

Sigma males also understand that failure is an inevitable part of the journey towards success. No one achieves greatness without experiencing setbacks and failures along the way. By embracing failure as a natural part of the process, Sigma males are able to stay focused on their goals and maintain their determination in the face of adversity.

Another key to successful risk-taking is mindset. Sigma males understand the importance of cultivating a growth mindset, which is characterized by a belief in one's ability to learn and grow from experience. This is in contrast to a fixed mindset, which is characterized by a belief that our skills and abilities are predetermined and cannot be changed.

By cultivating a growth mindset, Sigma males are able to approach risk-taking with a sense of curiosity and openness. They are willing to try new things and explore new opportunities, knowing that even if they fail, they will learn something valuable in the process.

Of course, there is always a risk of taking too many risks and experiencing a major setback. This is why it is important for Sigma males to be strategic and deliberate in their approach to risk-taking. They should carefully weigh the potential benefits and drawbacks of any given decision, and be willing to adjust their approach if things do not go as planned.

Overall, taking risks and embracing failure is a key part of the Sigma male mindset. By being willing to push beyond their comfort zone and explore new opportunities, Sigma males are able to achieve greatness and make a lasting impact on the world around them. Whether it is in their personal lives or their professional careers, Sigma males understand that the rewards of risk-taking far outweigh the risks.

9.7 Finding Balance in Your Life

Balance is an essential component of life. The sigma male understands the importance of balance and strives to achieve it in all aspects of his life. From personal relationships to career goals, the sigma male aims to balance his time, energy, and resources to achieve his desired level of independence and self-discovery.

Balancing Personal Relationships

Personal relationships are an important aspect of life. The sigma male understands the importance of maintaining healthy relationships with family, friends, and romantic partners. However, the sigma male also knows that too much emphasis on personal relationships can hinder his independence and self-discovery. Therefore, he strives to find a balance between his personal relationships and his individuality.

The sigma male values his personal relationships and invests time and energy into maintaining them. He prioritizes spending quality time with his loved ones, listening to their concerns and sharing his own. However, he also understands that he must maintain his independence and prioritize his own needs and desires.

The sigma male does not rely on his personal relationships to define his identity. He understands that he is an individual with unique goals, dreams, and aspirations. Therefore, he does not feel the need to conform to societal norms or expectations.

Balancing Career Goals

Career goals are a crucial aspect of a sigma male's life. He understands that his career is an essential component of his identity and success. However, the sigma male also recognizes that too much emphasis on his career can lead to burnout and hinder his personal growth.

Therefore, the sigma male strives to find a balance between his career goals and his personal life. He invests time and energy into his professional development, setting achievable goals and working diligently towards them. However, he also prioritizes his personal life and makes time for hobbies, interests, and relationships outside of work.

The sigma male does not define his success solely by his career achievements. He understands that there is more to life than a job title or salary. He values the importance of personal growth, self-discovery, and happiness.

Balancing Health and Wellness

Health and wellness are essential components of a sigma male's life. He understands that his physical and mental well-being is crucial to achieving his desired level of independence and self-discovery. Therefore, the sigma male strives to find a balance between his health and wellness goals and his personal and professional responsibilities.

The sigma male invests time and energy into maintaining his physical and mental health. He prioritizes regular exercise, healthy eating habits, and sufficient sleep. He also understands the importance of mental health and seeks support when necessary, whether it be through therapy or self-care practices.

The sigma male does not sacrifice his health and wellness goals for his personal or professional responsibilities. He understands that prioritizing his well-being will ultimately lead to greater success and fulfillment in all aspects of life.

Conclusion

Finding balance in life is a continuous journey for the sigma male. By prioritizing personal relationships, career goals, and health and wellness, the sigma male can achieve his desired level of independence and self-discovery. The sigma male understands the importance of staying true to himself and his unique goals and aspirations. He does not conform to societal norms or expectations and instead creates his path towards success and fulfillment. Balancing personal relationships, career goals, and health and wellness allows the sigma male to achieve his desired level of independence and self-discovery while living a fulfilling and meaningful life.

9.8 Letting Go of Societal Expectations

Letting go of societal expectations is a crucial step towards becoming a Sigma Male. As a Sigma Male, you recognize that society's expectations and norms aren't always aligned with your values, goals, and desires. You don't seek validation from others or conform to their expectations, but instead, you follow your own path and make your own rules.

One of the societal expectations that Sigma Males often struggle with is the pressure to conform to traditional gender roles. Society expects men to be dominant, aggressive, and competitive, while women are expected to be submissive, nurturing, and emotional. These expectations are deeply ingrained in our culture and reinforced by media, education, and socialization.

As a Sigma Male, you reject these gender roles and recognize that they limit your potential and freedom. You don't believe that masculinity is defined by physical strength, sexual conquests, or material success. Instead, you embrace a more holistic and authentic view of masculinity, one that values emotional intelligence, creativity, empathy, and introspection.

You don't feel the need to prove your masculinity or dominance to anyone, but instead, you focus on developing your own unique strengths and interests. You don't shy away from vulnerability or sensitivity, but instead, you embrace them as part of your humanity. You don't see women as inferior or subordinate, but instead, you respect and appreciate their diversity and complexity.

177

Another societal expectation that Sigma Males often reject is the pressure to conform to social norms and conventions. Society expects us to follow a certain path, such as getting a stable job, getting married, having kids, and accumulating wealth and status. While these goals may be desirable for some people, Sigma Males recognize that they aren't necessarily the only or best path to happiness and fulfillment.

You don't feel the need to fit into society's mold or live up to its expectations, but instead, you create your own path and pursue your own passions and goals. You don't measure your success by external standards or material possessions, but instead, you focus on your inner growth and self-discovery.

You may choose to live a minimalist lifestyle, travel the world, pursue unconventional careers, or create art and music. You may choose to live alone or with like-minded individuals, rather than conforming to traditional family structures. You may choose to prioritize your mental and physical health, rather than sacrificing them for the sake of productivity or success.

By letting go of societal expectations, Sigma Males free themselves from the pressure to conform or compete with others. They embrace their uniqueness and individuality, and recognize that their worth isn't determined by external standards or labels.

However, letting go of societal expectations isn't always easy or comfortable. Society's norms and expectations are deeply ingrained in our psyche, and breaking free from them can be challenging and risky. You may face criticism, rejection, or ostracism from others who don't understand or accept your choices and lifestyle.

Therefore, becoming a Sigma Male requires courage, resilience, and self-awareness. You need to be confident in your values, goals, and choices, and be able to communicate them effectively to others. You also need to be open-minded and adaptable, and be willing to learn from your experiences and mistakes.

One way to let go of societal expectations is to cultivate a mindset of detachment and non-attachment. Detachment means that you don't cling to your past, your identity, or your possessions, but instead, you let go of them and embrace change and uncertainty. Non-attachment means that you don't identify with your thoughts, emotions, or beliefs, but instead, you observe them impartially and let them pass.

By cultivating detachment and non-attachment, you free yourself from the limitations of your ego and the expectations of others. You become more flexible, resilient, and spontaneous, and you're able to adapt to new situations and challenges.

Another way to let go of societal expectations is to cultivate a growth mindset and a sense of purpose. A growth mindset means that you believe in your ability to learn, improve, and overcome obstacles, and that you embrace challenges as opportunities for growth. A sense of purpose means that you have a clear vision of your goals and values, and that you're motivated by a higher cause or mission.

By cultivating a growth mindset and a sense of purpose, you become more confident, resilient, and creative. You're able to face adversity with courage and optimism, and you're motivated by a sense of meaning and fulfillment.

In conclusion, letting go of societal expectations is a crucial step towards becoming a Sigma Male. By rejecting traditional gender roles and social norms, Sigma Males free themselves from the pressure to conform or compete with others. They embrace their uniqueness and individuality, and recognize that their worth isn't determined by external standards or labels.

However, letting go of societal expectations isn't always easy or comfortable. It requires courage, resilience, and self-awareness. Sigma Males need to cultivate a mindset of detachment and non-attachment, a growth mindset, and a sense of purpose, in order to thrive in a world that often values conformity and mediocrity.

So, if you're on the path to becoming a Sigma Male, remember to let go of societal expectations, embrace your uniqueness and individuality, and follow your own path and purpose. You have the potential to create a life of freedom, creativity, and fulfillment, and to inspire others to do the same.

9.9 Creating Your Own Path to Success

As a Sigma Male, you understand the importance of independence and self-discovery. You know that success is not just about achieving predetermined goals, but also about finding your own path and defining success on your own terms. In order to achieve this, there are several steps you can take to create your own path to success.

1. Define Your Own Success

The first step to creating your own path to success is defining what success means to you. This means taking the time to reflect on your values, goals, and priorities. What do you truly want out of life? What are your long-term and short-term goals? What are your personal and professional priorities?

Once you have a clear understanding of what success means to you, you can start to work towards achieving it. Keep in mind that success is not a one-size-fits-all concept. What is considered successful for one person may not be the same for another. This is why it's important to define your own success and work towards achieving it on your own terms.

2. Take Ownership of Your Life

As a Sigma Male, you understand the importance of taking ownership of your life. This means being accountable for your actions and taking responsibility for your own success. You cannot rely on others to create your path to success for you. You must take control of your own life and make the necessary changes to achieve your goals.

This may mean making some difficult decisions, such as leaving a job that no longer fulfills you or ending a toxic relationship. It may also mean taking risks and stepping outside of your comfort zone. But by taking ownership of your life, you will be able to create a path to success that is truly your own.

3. Embrace Failure

Failure is a natural part of the journey towards success. As a Sigma Male, you understand that failure is not the end, but rather an opportunity to learn and grow. Embracing failure means accepting that you will make mistakes along the way, but using those mistakes as a learning experience to help you move forward.

Instead of being afraid of failure, embrace it as an opportunity to learn and grow. Take calculated risks and don't be afraid to try new things. Remember, the most successful people in the world have failed many times before achieving success.

4. Focus on Your Strengths

In order to create your own path to success, it's important to focus on your strengths. This means identifying what you are good at and using those skills to your advantage. It's easy to get caught up in trying to improve our weaknesses, but focusing on our strengths is what will set us apart and help us achieve success.

Take the time to identify your strengths and find ways to use them in your personal and professional life. This may mean pursuing a career that aligns with your strengths or starting a business that utilizes your unique skills.

5. Surround Yourself with Positive Influences

The people we surround ourselves with have a significant impact on our lives. Surrounding yourself with positive influences can help you stay motivated and focused on your path to success. These positive influences may be mentors, friends, family, or colleagues who share your values and support your goals.

On the other hand, negative influences can hold you back and hinder your progress. These may be people who are unsupportive of your goals or who bring negativity into your life. It's important to recognize these negative influences and distance yourself from them as much as possible.

6. Continuously Learn and Grow

The path to success is not a destination, but rather a journey. As a Sigma Male, you understand the importance of continuously learning and growing. This means seeking out new experiences, expanding your knowledge, and taking on new challenges.

Continuously learning and growing will not only help you achieve your goals but will also help you become a more well-rounded and fulfilled person. This may mean pursuing further education, attending seminars and conferences, or simply reading books and articles related to your interests.

7. Be Patient and Persistent

Creating your own path to success is not a quick or easy process. It takes patience and persistence to achieve your goals. There will be setbacks and obstacles along the way, but by staying patient and persistent, you will be able to overcome them and continue on your path to success.

Remember, success is not a destination but a journey. By staying patient and persistent, you will be able to enjoy the journey and appreciate the process as much as the end result.

In Conclusion

Creating your own path to success as a Sigma Male is about defining success on your own terms, taking ownership of your life, embracing failure, focusing on your strengths, surrounding yourself with positive influences, continuously learning and growing, and being patient and persistent. By taking these steps, you will be able to create a path to success that is truly your own and achieve your goals on your own terms.

Printed in Great Britain
by Amazon

62206987R00111